Lars Hanson and Greta Garbo in *The Atonement of Gösta Berling*.

SWEDISH FILM CLASSICS

A Pictorial Survey of 25 Films from 1913 to 1957

by
ALEKSANDER KWIATKOWSKI

Published in association with
Svenska Filminstitutet, Stockholm
by
Dover Publications, Inc., New York

ACKNOWLEDGMENTS

Among those who helped me greatly in preparing this book I would like to mention film historians Bengt Forslund, Leif Furhammar, Nils Hugo Geber, Bo Heurling and Gösta Werner, as well as the whole editorial board of *Svensk filmografi*, particularly Staffan Grönberg. Christian Wirsén and Olle Rosberg of the Swedish Film Institute helped me in the selection of pictures.

Last but not least, I would like to thank the representatives of the two co-publishers of the book, Stanley Appelbaum of Dover Publications and Lars Åhlander of the Swedish Film Institute, whose zealous alertness helped to correct some false notions in the text. If any mistakes still remain, they are all mine.

A. K.

Published in Canada by General Publishing Company, Ltd., 30 Lesmill Road, Don Mills, Toronto, Ontario.
Published in the United Kingdom by Constable and Company, Ltd., 10 Orange Street, London, WC2H 7EG.

Swedish Film Classics: A Pictorial Survey of 25 Films from 1913 to 1957 is a new work, first published in 1983 by Dover Publications, Inc., in association with Svenska Filminstitutet, Stockholm.

Manufactured in the United States of America
Dover Publications, Inc., 180 Varick Street, New York, N.Y. 10014

Library of Congress Cataloging in Publication Data

Kwiatkowski, Aleksander.
  Swedish film classics.

  1. Moving-pictures—Sweden—Pictorial works.
I. Svenska Filminstitutet. II. Title.
PN1993.5.S8K9   791.43'75   81-17392
ISBN 0-486-24304-4 (pbk.)   AACR2

CONTENTS

SIX DECADES OF SWEDISH FILM, 1896–1957

Swedish film production originated not in Stockholm but in Kristianstad, a city on the Baltic side of the nation's southernmost tip. These first attempts were made in 1907 by Franz G. Wiberg, but the only feature film he managed to produce, *The Man Who Takes Care of the Villain* (Han som klara boven), has never been theatrically released. That same year another film company was founded in Kristianstad, AB Svenska Biografteatern, usually referred to in the shorter form Svenska Bio. It was to move to Stockholm five years later. From 1909 its head and its main driving force was the Göteborg photographer Charles Magnusson (1878–1948). As early as 1905/1906 he had produced some short current-events films on Sweden's west coast and had filmed the coronation ceremony and celebrations held in Norway at that time. With Magnusson at the helm, Svenska Bio soon surged ahead. The result was a whole series of films patterned after the French *film d'art*, painstakingly crafted to the extent that the limited running time allowed. Extremely stage-oriented versions of literary works were directed for the firm by Gustaf Lindén, a theatrical director from Stockholm.

Meanwhile, other production firms were making noteworthy contributions. The film version of the musical folk play *The People of Värmland* (Värmlänningarna), made in 1910 by the Malmö producer Frans Lundberg, was the most successful item among this group (the Swedish cinema has, from its very start, always been faithful to its roots, deeply set in national folklore). In 1911/12 N. P. Nilsson—a former horse dealer, then a Stockholm movie theater owner, eventually a film producer—undertook such ambitious projects as Strindberg's *Miss Julie* (Fröken Julie) and *The Father* (Fadren) for the film company Orientaliska Teatern.

But Svenska Bio kept the lead. Magnusson's momentum and energy are perhaps best illustrated by his sending a film crew headed by cameraman Julius Jaenzon (1885–1961) across the ocean in 1911 to shoot scenes of street traffic in New York City and do some filming at Niagara Falls. These shots were included in some early pictures made by Svenska Bio. Eager to match the flourishing Danish film production of the day, Magnusson also laid the foundations for the new eruption of talent in the Swedish silent film. In 1912 he hired the theatrical actor-directors Victor Sjöström (1879–1960; called Seastrom when he worked in Hollywood) and Mauritz Stiller (1883–1928). After a period of training at the new Lidingö studio near Stockholm, these two men, along with camerman Julius Jaenzon, became responsible for the most spectacular successes of Swedish film art.

Another interesting film production center started in Göteborg at Hasselblad's, the firm of the renowned camera manufacturer. Between 1914 and 1917, with director Georg af Klercker and actor Carl Barcklind as its greatest assets, the company produced quality comedies and thrillers. Hasselblad's ambition was to abolish the virtual domination of the European film market by the Nordisk Films Compagni of Denmark (called Nordisk for short) and Pathé Frères of France. The new Swedish motion-picture company founded in 1918, the Skandia, had as shareholders Pathé, Hasselblad and the distribution company Victoria Film AB. A year later, as a result of a merger between Skandia and Svenska Bio, the new firm AB Svensk Filmindustri (abbreviated SF) was established.

Svenska Bio (from 1919, Svensk Filmindustri) did succeed in supplanting Nordisk on international markets. Its conscious policy of limiting production to only a few significant pictures a year yielded a unique series of masterpieces within the relatively short period from 1916 to 1924.

Another policy of the firm, the choice of subjects from the treasury of national literature, proved a most fortunate one. The chief resource was the works of Selma Lagerlöf (1858–1940), Nobel Prize winner for literature in 1909. Miss Lagerlöf was not as obliging to moviemakers as August Strindberg (1849–1912) had been; a few months before his death he wrote to the earliest authors of films based on his plays: "You may film as many of my works as you wish." Whenever a book by Selma Lagerlöf was to be filmed, she scrutinized the project thoroughly in advance, though not in an unfriendly manner. Svenska Bio signed a five-year contract with the authoress committing itself to make one of her books into a picture every year. First came *The Girl from the Marsh Croft*[1] (Tösen från Stormyrtorpet), 1917. Soon afterward, Sjöström proceeded to adapt the two volumes of her folk epic *Jerusalem* for the screen, and over the following two years he produced three full-length pictures, having adapted in all only 100 pages of the 700 in the novel. Further chapters were to be processed into film in the Twenties by Gustaf Molander, after Sjöström and Stiller had departed for Hollywood.

Mauritz Stiller also used literary texts as a basis for his films, giving preference to lighter subjects—comedy and suspense. Whereas Sjöström's adaptations remained completely faithful to the original works as well as to the environments he was reconstructing, Stiller made free use of the literary material in order to achieve his own impressive visions, frequently associated with a very personal, emotional approach to the subject he was handling. Sjöström—to quote the director Benjamin Christensen—was imitating "the very rhythm of life." Stiller, an immigrant from Finland lacking permanent roots to some extent and differing from Sjöström in character, mood and the aims of his art, elaborated the surface texture of life. The French film historians Bardèche and Brasillach saw Sjöström as a poet, Stiller as a painter, of the screen.

The close relation of Swedish films to literature and their firm setting in national reality and tradition gave them another distinguishing trait at that early period and later became the specific characteristic of Scandinavian filmmaking in general. This was the integration with Northern nature, which was sometimes used merely as a beautiful background for presenting the story, but often as a dramatic element too, menacing and demanding, actively interfering with human existence. Furthermore—with even more emphasis in the years to come—the natural setting was

---

[1] A literal translation of the Swedish title is "The Girl from Great Marsh (Tenant) Farm." Besides the distribution title given above, there is a less correct one, *The Lass from the Stormy Croft.*

seen as a perfect background for the struggle inside man's psyche and its collisions with mystical, ritual and religious forces. In their approach to nature as well as in their attitude to literary texts, Sjöström and Stiller were entirely different, although each of them worked with the third principal creator of Swedish film art in the period of its greatness, Julius Jaenzon.

Sjöström and Stiller were, of course, not the only directors in Sweden. Prominent among the others was John Brunius (1884–1937), pillar of the Skandia company and director of *Synnöve Solbakken* (1919), based on the Norwegian novel by Bjørnstjerne Bjørnson, a picture that was appreciated all over Scandinavia and was particularly successful in Norway.[2] During the peak period 1916–1924, the Danish directors Fritz Magnussen, Lau Lauritzen, Carl Theodor Dreyer, Benjamin Christensen and Robert Dinesen, the Norwegian Egil Eide and Finland's Konrad Tallroth all made significant contributions to the Swedish cinema. Other Swedes guarding the honor and continuity of Swedish production in the period before the departure of Sjöström and Stiller were the actor-directors Carl Barcklind, Rune Carlsten, Ivan Hedquist and Sigurd Wallén. In these glorious days of the early Twenties, the Swedish cinema possessed three filmmaking plants. At the time, SF was controlled by finance tycoon Ivar Kreuger, a heavy investor in film.

The triumphant procession of the best Swedish pictures through European and world movie houses unfortunately ended almost as abruptly as it had started. Sjöström's *The Phantom Carriage* and Stiller's later pictures appealed to the educated, sophisticated public, but the mass audience, when faced with a choice between the easily digestible, light Hollywood productions and the serious, grim Scandinavian art, soon turned away from Swedish films. Under the circumstances, Stiller's *Erotikon* and the films Sjöström made in cooperation with writer Hjalmar Bergman—in particular the Renaissance drama *Mortal Clay/Love's Crucible* (Vem dömer?) of 1921—were an attempt to regain lost territory and to give Swedish production a cosmopolitan profile. But this abandonment of national literature and tradition proved to be a disastrous divorce from the creative inspiration that had allowed the best of Swedish work to attain a truly universal dimension.

The artistic decline of the Swedish cinema coincided with the departure of the most prominent directors and actors for Hollywood. Sjöström's original one-year contract with Goldwyn was meant to give him a new creative experience and was linked to a bilateral agreement concerning the Swedish distribution of his pictures made in America. But eventually he spent six years in the States, only returning to his home country at the outset of the talkie era. Stiller did not have the same success; in Hollywood he fought a futile battle for artistic independence against the omnipotent major producers. When only two of his pictures proved to be fairly profitable, he was forced to take on such jobs as directing episodes and sequences to be incorporated into other directors' films. Gravely ill, he returned to Stockholm in 1928, and died there in November of that same year. Sjöström took care of him to the very end.

Starting in 1923, many other outstanding Scandinavian film people emigrated to Hollywood. The cinema boom at home was over and the world capital of filmmaking offered not only princely salaries but also the promise of complete creative freedom for film artists who had already achieved position and renown. Disillusionment with the industrialized production methods at the "dream factory" resulted in many a personal drama. The directors Victor Sjöström, Mauritz Stiller, Benjamin Christensen and Svend Gade and the actors Greta Garbo, Lars Hanson, Einar Hanson, Betty Nansen, Karin Molander and Nils Asther all gathered in California; for a short period, writer Hjalmar Bergman joined them, trying to get settled. Other newcomers from Europe arriving in Hollywood in the same period included Ernst Lubitsch, Dimitri Buchowetzki, F. W. Murnau, Pola Negri, Emil Jannings and Conrad Veidt; gradually taking exclusive control of the world's film market, Hollywood persistently drained Europe of its greatest talents.

The directors who remained in the Swedish studios had worked until then in the shadow of the great masters, and now some script writers took to directing as well. No wonder they began by imitating former successes. Gustaf Molander, who had written the scripts for many of Sjöström's films, continued the ongoing series of films based on Selma Lagerlöf's *Jerusalem* with the two pictures *Ingmar's Inheritance* (Ingmarsarvet) and *To the Orient* (Till Österland), both 1925. Another former screenplay author, Ragnar Hyltén-Cavallius, together with Paul Merzbach, who came from Germany, proceeded in the mid-Twenties to shoot cosmopolitan comedies and dramas, mainly in coproduction with German companies and with an international cast performing.

The hopes that these rather trite and paltry pictures might succeed proved almost entirely vain. Nor did attempts to produce monumental costume spectacles conquer the international market, though the good work of John Brunius deserves special recognition.

Outstanding even in this period was the current that continued to draw inspiration from folk tradition. Its leading director, Gustaf Edgren (1895–1954), cultivated rural romanticism and became the pioneer of the comedy trend that was to gather strength in later Swedish films. The folk hero was played in the earliest of these pictures by Fridolf Rhudin, the predecessor of the most popular comedy character of the Fifties, Åsa-Nisse.

Swedish cinema entered the sound era well prepared both technically and financially. Experienced companies such as SF and new ones kept the production machinery going, and the number of new films reached more than twenty a year. These solid financial foundations were closely connected with declining ambitions and artistry. The Swedish film no longer had the desire or the ability to impress the world with original achievements. What was left, as venomous critics commented, was a traditionalism that took no financial risks but pampered public taste, which had been effectively lowered to the most undemanding common denominator.

The chief distinctions between the types of films produced depended on the kind of alcohol the protagonists enjoyed and the clothes they wore. Champagne, cognac and meals on silver services—this was the world of Svensk Filmindustri and that of the leading director of elegant dramas, Gustaf Molander. Grits in a pot, vodka and beer were the identifying marks of the newly founded Europa Film, which specialized in folk farces starring such popular comedians as Edvard Persson and Fridolf Rhudin. Oscillating between the two extremes were some smaller studios whose output exemplified the restlessness of the middle class, ambitious for promotion to the aristocracy or upper bourgeoisie

---

[2]Just as successful was the 1919 film version of Bjørnson's *A Dangerous Courtship* (Et farligt frieri). Of course, Sjöström's great *Terje Vigen* of 1916 had also been based on a Norwegian work, a poem by Henrik Ibsen.

while their financial means were more in line with the beer-consuming lower classes. "Pilsnerfilm" was the nickname given to the most numerous group of pictures, the indiscriminate farces derived from the tradition of open-air performances in the so-called bush theaters. The early Thirties were a period of crisis not for film art alone, but also for the stage. Audiences had a preference for comedies set in a rural or provincial environment, with a simplified sense of humor and stereotyped characters. Both stage and film versions of that kind of entertainment enjoyed success.

This general decline in artistic level surprisingly coexisted with an active cultural and social elite, which was apparently unable to shape public opinion as it wished. Nevertheless, dogged attacks on the sheer profit motivation of commercial filmmaking came from sophisticated critics and writers on esthetics who still remembered the years of Swedish film greatness, as well as from social activists who saw the vulgar farces as a threat to decency and an encouragement to immorality, heavy drinking and violence.

Although film art itself was lethargic in the Thirties, several operations of lasting benefit for the film world had their origins in this period: the first steps taken by the film-club movement, modest attempts at opening art theaters, the foundation of the Film Academy with the germs of a motion-picture archive and museum, and eventually the first parliamentary discussions on the subject of film culture.

Perhaps this undercurrent of cultural activities was among the essential factors that made it possible in the next decade for Swedish films to move out of their blind alley and enter a second period of glory.

The political situation was also largely responsible for the Swedish cinema's rebirth in the World War II years. The country's relative isolation as a result of its neutrality caused a substantial decline in imports of foreign films. This situation gave new possibilities for expanding domestic production, and sufficient ambition was generated to bring it up to a high level. Personnel changes in the major producing companies also played a role. The new head of SF was Carl Anders Dymling, who made veteran Victor Sjöström his artistic supervisor. Another factor harking back to the first period of Swedish film excellence was a renewed interest in serious literature. In 1942 Sandrews Studios made critic and historian Rune Waldekranz (b. 1911) its chief of production,

and Terrafilm's ambitious program was headed by former critic, film-club activist and film director Lorens Marmstedt (1908–1966). Both of these men belonged to the generation that had demanded reform back in the Thirties.

Concurrent with the aims of such men and the generally inspiring atmosphere that prevailed was a turning away from the imitative, no-conflict image of life that had confined the Swedish cinema within provincial boundaries and a new investigation of the universality inherent in national artistic resources. International distribution expanded as Swedish films once again became more meaningful for the whole world.

The boom established during the war—an annual average of nearly forty pictures, an unheard-of number for a country with a population of six million—lasted until the late Forties, encouraging producers to take greater financial risks and do more artistic experimenting. And certainly for film auteurs such as Alf Sjöberg and Ingmar Bergman, the venture has not been inconsiderable.

On the other hand, during the late Forties and the Fifties the Swedish film largely continued to be a local, provincial art, in much the same way that it had been during the Thirties. But the crisis was now not only of a cultural and artistic kind. It was a financial crisis, too, chiefly generated by the government's entertainment taxes, which at times were as high as 39%. This made the Swedish film companies financially shaky, and in 1951 they announced a year-long halt in production. During this year only a few films were made (among them *One Summer of Happiness* by Arne Mattsson). The government tried to alleviate this situation through several investigations and a partial diminishing of the tax burden.

Swedish film production as a whole decreased during this period from the rather exaggerated number of films released during the extraordinarily favorable war period—more than forty pictures a year—to the more realistic figure of about thirty. After the production halt, the industry was to meet other problems, such as the introduction of new techniques; the first Swedish color feature was made in 1946, and Agascope, a Swedish system of CinemaScope, came into use in this period. The triumphant offensive of television in the late Fifties led to the death of many cinemas and at the same time meant an increase in production costs. This catastrophic situation was to be remedied in 1963 by a film reform and by the foundation of the Swedish Film Institute. But that is another story, beyond the scope of this book.

INGEBORG HOLM

(Swedish title: "Ingeborg Holm." British title: "Margaret Day.")

Produced 1913 by AB Svenska Biografteatern. Released November 3, 1913.

Director: Victor Sjöström. Screenplay (based on the play by Nils Krook): Victor Sjöström. Camera: Henrik Jaenzon.

CAST: Hilda Borgström (*Ingeborg Holm*); Aron Lindgren (*Sven Holm, her husband, and Erik Holm their son, as an adult*); Eric Lindholm (*employee in shop*); Georg Grönroos (*poorhouse superintendent*); William Larsson (*police officer*); Richard Lund (*physician*); Carl Barcklind (*house doctor*).

SYNOPSIS & COMMENTARY: In 1913 social consciousness was neither a new topic in films nor limited to Sweden. Nevertheless this mature film, focused on strong social criticism, came about more or less coincidentally. The contract of outstanding actress Hilda Borgström with Svenska Bio was running out. The manager of the firm, Charles Magnusson, then decided to use her talent in one more film role. A young director, Victor Sjöström, who had been working in the cinema for only a year, fished out of his desk an old and partly forgotten screenplay adapted from a stage play that had been written by Nils Krook. Krook, headmaster of a business school in Helsingborg (southern Sweden) and member of a local council for social welfare, had based his *Ingeborg Holm* on real experiences. It was fairly successful on stage (in 1907 it was adapted for a production by Sjöström himself), but in that era of predominantly society melodramas, the idea of a screen version interested neither Nordisk nor Svenska Bio, to whom Krook offered his text. At last, the possibility of casting a well-known actress in a role suited to her powers got Magnusson to make up his mind and take the risk.

The film begins by showing a genuine Swedish family idyll. The Holms—husband, wife and three children—have come out to their allotment garden to spend Sunday. They hoist the flag and potter about the garden. The children are dressed in white. The scene has peace and harmony. It then appears that the husband has had a letter from a bank granting him credit to open a grocery store. He has been thrifty and hard-working. Everything in these scenes is genuine and real. After the introductory idyll the perspective of the story darkens quickly. The Holm family is still only fitting up the shop when the husband has a hemorrhage of the lungs and is bedridden. His wife nurses him. A dishonest assistant helps to undermine their finances. The husband dies. Ingeborg is left alone to work for their daily bread. But she is not able to keep by herself the store her husband started, because of her inexperience and the assistant's theft. She goes bankrupt. According to the law, in such cases the children are farmed out to others and Ingeborg Holm has to move to the poorhouse. One day she learns that her daughter Valborg has fallen ill. She sneaks out at night from the poorhouse to visit her child. The police are on her trail but a friendly farmer and his wife help her. However, the police catch up with her at the very moment when she reaches the house where the sick child lives. She is allowed to see her child before being brought back to the poorhouse. Her unhappy experiences affect Ingeborg's mind and she loses her reason. Her youngest child no longer recognizes her. As a symbol of her lost life Ingeborg holds a bundle of rags in her arms, deluding herself that this is her child. In an epilogue, Erik, the son of Ingeborg, now a grown-up man and a sailor, returns from the sea to Sweden after many years. He traces his mother and goes to her. By means of an old photograph he succeeds in making himself recognized by his mother. The shock presumably helps Ingeborg to regain her sanity. This "happy ending," however, is by no means meant as a compensation for the real unhappiness that has preceded, and cannot be treated as an easy solution.

Hilda Borgström (1871–1953) was at the time not only the best-paid film star after Asta Nielsen, with a salary of 5,000 Swedish crowns for thirty days of shooting, but also one of the preeminent actresses in the early years of film. Her restrained acting made the film a success and is the main reason for the strong impact it still has today.

Ingeborg Holm, generally considered as the harbinger of the Swedish school, was forgotten for many years. It was rediscovered in the Fifties by film-archive and film-club audiences. This specialized and often blasé public found that Hilda Borgström had succeeded in overcoming the sentimentality of the script and had created a real picture of human destiny, played against a thoroughly documentary background showing the activities of "philanthropic" institutions. The criticism of these activities, and the protest against inhuman laws which permitted taking children from their mother, was another value of the film, which provoked hot social debate.

Victor Sjöström treated the subject and the environment with ease and assuredness. Some of the motifs from this early movie, with their clear statement of social values, were to find a place in his later films, especially in his masterpiece, *The Phantom Carriage*. But with *Ingeborg Holm* Sjöström had already proven his directorial maturity.

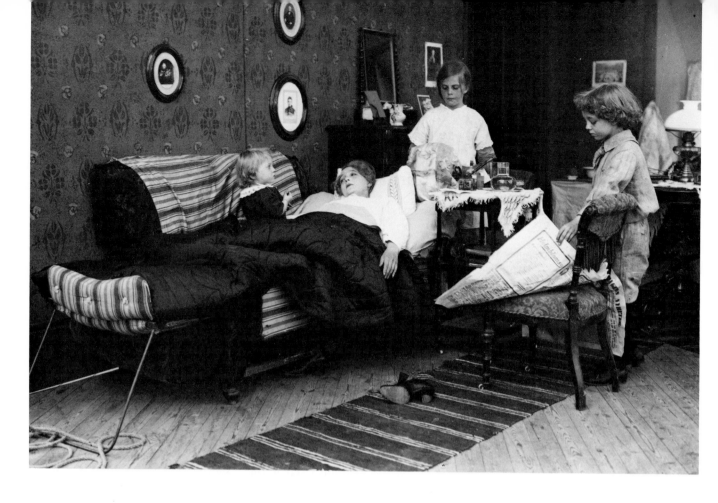

ABOVE: Ingeborg Holm prostrated by her husband's death. BELOW: Ingeborg Holm moves into the poorhouse.

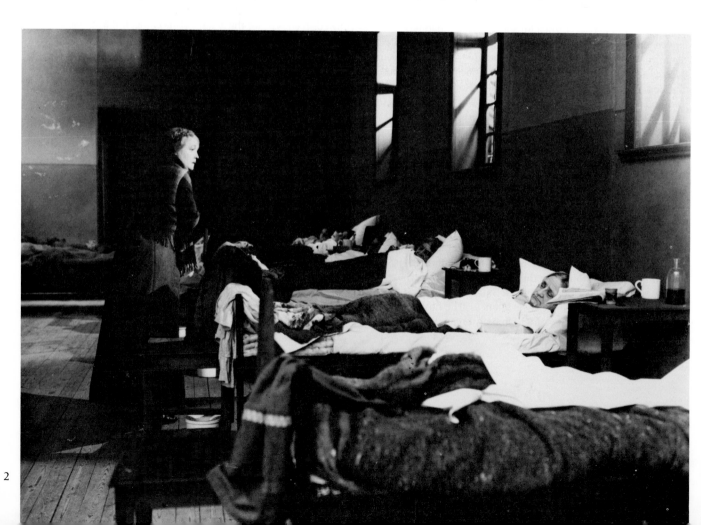

ABOVE: She attempts to escape from the poorhouse. BELOW: The poorhouse superintendent berates her.

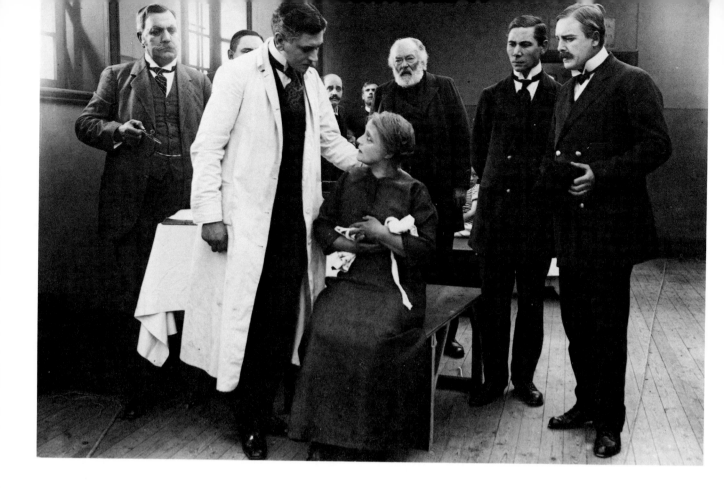

ABOVE: The poorhouse doctor has hopes for her recovery. BELOW: She is reunited with her sailor son.

LOVE AND JOURNALISM

(Swedish title: "Kärlek och journalistik.")

Produced 1916 by AB Svenska Biografteatern. Released August 14, 1916.

Director: Mauritz Stiller. Screenplay: Harriet Bloch. Camera: Gustaf Boge. Art Director: Axel Esbensen.

CAST: Richard Lund (*Dr. Eric Bloomée, a scientist*); Jenny Tschernichin-Larsson (*his mother*); Karin Molander (*Hertha Weye, a journalist*); Stina Berg (*Stina, the housekeeper*); Gucken Cederborg (*Rosika Amunds*); Julius Hälsig (*a newspaperman*).

SYNOPSIS & COMMENTARY: Sjöström and Stiller's first years as film directors with Svenska Bio were a good training period. The differences in their style and approach to filmmaking were already in evidence: Sjöström leaned toward serious, dramatic subjects, whereas Stiller—even though he already had to his credit a few psychological high-society dramas and a few thrillers patterned after Danish movies—showed a preference for farce and comedy sparkling with his own sophisticated sense of humor. Of the thirty-two pictures he made between 1912 and 1916, prints of only one are available, *Love and Journalism*. The picture is an evident forerunner of the comedy style that was to become a Stiller trademark.

The famous explorer Dr. Eric Bloomée has returned from an expedition to the South Pole. In spite of all attempts to keep his arrival secret, the news has spread widely and all the city newspapers would give anything to get an interview with the famous man. But all fail to meet him at the railway station, and the only reporter who gets to the Bloomées' home is fended off by the old housekeeper. Then a young female journalist, Hertha Weye, chances to see an ad placed in the paper by Mrs. Bloomée, Eric's mother, who is looking for a young girl to help her with the housekeeping. Hertha disguises herself as a 16-year-old, applies

for the job and gets it. While working in the house, she uses the opportunity to study Eric's documents from the expedition, and eventually gets her article ready. But for an interview she needs some pictures and a portrait too, and when she tries to take them, she is caught red-handed by the housekeeper. Eric, however, hardly believes in her guilt, as she has made an impression upon him as a woman too. In order to discover her identity, he checks the addresses of her references, which are all false. After he catches sight of her at a restaurant as an elegant lady, he learns about her being a journalist. Meanwhile, Hertha has fallen in love with Eric too. Her feelings for him give her a bad conscience, and after some hesitation she tears the manuscript of her interview to bits. At the same moment he pays a visit to her. He is very serious and blames her for a great many things. She defends herself as well as she can, but suddenly he casts off his mask, and they kiss and get engaged. The editor of the newspaper loses both the interview and his lady journalist, but Hertha gets the man she wants, and Mrs. Bloomée gets back her former maid as a daughter-in-law.

Contemporaries thought *Love and Journalism* was a Danish-inspired film, a presentation of society life meant merely to entertain audiences, with no attention to social problems. What was new in the picture, however, was the realistic situations the characters were shown in, situations with which the spectators could identify. Stiller's narration is purely visual (only twenty-five intertitles in the whole picture), streamlined, lucidly carrying the plot forward. He was to improve the model of such comedies in collaboration with scriptwriter Gustaf Molander, from the films about Thomas Graal to *Erotikon* (all of these with Karin Molander). The model of a feature-length comedy that was developed during this period would remain vital for years and would be successfully duplicated in series in the cinema of the Thirties and Forties. The plot of *Love and Journalism*, for instance, was repeated in 1937 in Tay Garnett's *Love Is News*.

ABOVE: The journalists fail to meet the scientist Eric Bloomée at the railway station. BELOW: Stina, the housekeeper, fends off an aggressive journalist.

ABOVE: Mrs. Bloomée and her son find that they need an extra maid. BELOW: Hertha Weye, a disguised lady journalist hired as a servant, enjoys breakfast with Stina.

ABOVE: The false servant is caught red-handed while scanning the scientist's papers. BELOW: Hertha comes back to Bloomée's house to become a wife and daughter-in-law.

TERJE VIGEN

(Swedish title: "Terje Vigen." English-language title: "A Man There Was.")

Produced 1916 by AB Svenska Biografteatern. Released January 29, 1917.

Director: Victor Sjöström. Screenplay (based on the poem by Henrik Ibsen): Gustaf Molander. Camera: Julius Jaenzon. Art Director: Axel Esbensen.

CAST: Victor Sjöström (*Terje Vigen*); Bergliot Husberg (*his wife*); August Falck (*the Lord*); Edith Erastoff (*the Lady*).

SYNOPSIS & COMMENTARY: The spring of 1916 was a critical time for Victor Sjöström, both personally (he was then divorced from actress Lili Beck) and professionally. Perhaps he was dissatisfied with directing a whole string of films that were stereotyped and meaningless (except for *Ingeborg Holm* of 1913). In the fall, upon his return to the Lidingö studio, he undertook his most ambitious project to date, one that entailed a modification of Svenska Bio's production policy: the filming of a poem by Henrik Ibsen.

The plot of "Terje Vigen" (published in 1862), a work that had risen to the rank of a national epic, is set in the period 1807–1814, after the British had introduced the continental blockade during the Napoleonic wars. Most painfully affected by the blockade was Norway, and regardless of its close trade relations with England the country was forced to side with Napoleon. This brought misery and hunger on the Norwegian people. The hero of the poem is Terje Vigen who, desirous of saving his wife and young daughter from starvation, sets out to sea in a small, frail boat to get food from Denmark. On his way back he is caught by a British corvette. The vessel's young commander, indifferent to the unfortunate man's pleading, sends him to prison. After spending five years in prison, Terje is released and returns home to find his house occupied by strangers, his wife and daughter dead. (This part of the story is told in a flashback.)

A few more years pass. One day Terje, a skilled sea pilot, happens to rescue the passengers of a yacht during a storm. They would otherwise have crashed against rocks. In the owner of the yacht he recognizes the officer who once doomed his family to starvation. The lives of the officer (an English lord) and his family are now in Terje's hands. During the dramatic culmination, contradictory feelings—the urge for revenge and the awareness of the duty to save one's fellow man—are reflected on the protagonist's face. Terje controls himself and repays the British lord with nobleness and generosity. The yacht sails off, hoisting the Norwegian banner in a farewell salute.

Terje Vigen was a turning point in Swedish motion-picture production. From that point on at Svenska Bio, Magnusson's motto was to make only a few films, but well selected and thoroughly prepared ones. *Terje Vigen* was the start of a series of adaptations of masterpieces of Scandinavian literature. It was also the first film in which advantage was consciously taken of the dramatic and poetic values of Northern nature. Locations began to participate in the action as an element of decisive impact on the characters' fate. Sjöström did not strive for any kind of elaborate visual style but brought out the simplicity and expressiveness contained in the subject. In his 1960 work *La grande aventure du cinéma suédois*, film historian Jean Béranger wrote: "Thus almost the whole plot developed on the sea—a sea, now calm now stormy, that constantly dominated the entire narrative with its very presence. Confronted with its boundless space, the evil inclinations of men, their pernicious fighting prompted by arbitrary and temporary patriotic goals, took on a wildly absurd semblance. For the first time actors were set against an immense natural background in which they seemed to be behaving like wretched little ants. Only the gesture of final forgiveness brought them into harmony with the greatness of the sea, corresponding closely in its very clemency with the calming of the waves after the paroxysm of the storm."

The film was a tremendous success, both critically and financially. It was well received all over Europe, even in England, despite its anti-British aspects—which were magnified by German propaganda during the First World War. *Terje Vigen* was also the first Swedish film reviewed in Swedish newpapers. The review was written by the theater critic Bo Bergman, later a member of the Swedish Academy of Literature.

Sjöström's personal problems also found a happy solution. Edith Erastoff, who appeared in the role of the British lady, became the director's wife two years later. In the next outstanding work of the Swedish school, *The Outlaw and His Wife*, they were to act together again.

ABOVE: Terje curses the elements after losing his family. (Then the flashback begins.) BELOW: As Terje Vigen returns from Denmark with food, his boat is shot at by a British corvette.

ABOVE: Terje is taken prisoner by the British military. BELOW: Terje serving his prison term.

ABOVE: The yacht of the British lord is caught in a storm. BELOW: His life is now in Terje's hands.

THE OUTLAW AND HIS WIFE

(Swedish title "Berg-Ejvind och hans hustru" [literally, "Berg-Ejvind and His Wife"]. Original U.S. distribution title: "You and I." Original British distribution title: "Love, the Only Law.")

Produced 1917 by AB Svenska Biografteatern. Released January 1, 1918.

Director: Victor Sjöström. Screenplay (based on the play by Jóhann Sigurjónsson): Victor Sjöström and Sam Ask. Camera: Julius Jaenzon. Art Director: Axel Esbensen.

CAST: Victor Sjöström (*Berg-Ejvind*); Edith Erastoff (*Halla, his wife*); John Ekman (*Arnes, the sheep thief*); Nils Aréhn (*Björn Bergsteinsson*).

SYNOPSIS & COMMENTARY: Sjöström's next ambitious project was to adapt a play by Iceland's Jóhann Sigurjónsson, *The Outlaw and His Wife*. The plot is laid in Iceland in the nineteenth century. Halla, a rich widow, takes on Kari as a hired man on her farm and falls in love with him. Halla's brother-in-law, Björn, who wants to seize her property, discovers that Kari is really a fugitive from justice, the sheep thief Berg-Ejvind. Threatened with imprisonment, Ejvind runs for his life to hide in the mountains, taking Halla along. They spend five years there in happy coexistence with nature, bringing up their baby daughter. During their dramatic struggle against Björn's flunkeys who have tracked them down, they lose their child: Halla would rather throw her little girl over a cliff than abandon her to the people she despises. The two exiles find shelter by escaping higher up the mountains. Many years later, united by their mutual love and a desire for freedom stronger than death, they perish in a snowstorm.

Sigurjónsson's play had been directed by Sjöström on the stage in Göteborg back in 1911, with Sjöström himself in the leading male role. This association may have led to his occasionally flamboyant acting in the film, and to the clear division of the picture into parts, each determined by unity of time and place: on Halla's farm, in the mountains before the child's death, in the snowstorm. The critics' response after the premiere was unanimously favorable, often enthusiastic; it is only recently that these minor shortcomings have been noted. Sjöström succeeded, particularly in scenes shot in very difficult conditions in the mountains of Lapland near the Norwegian border (an expedition to authentic Icelandic locations was impossible because German submarines prowled the North Sea and the Atlantic), in presenting human destinies against the background of life-giving nature. This austere background, chosen with full awareness, emphasized the hard lot of people who by their own choice had placed themselves beyond the law and beyond society.

The Outlaw and His Wife, to an even greater extent than *Terje Vigen*, brought Swedish films onto the international forum. The film's success, greatest in France, the country leading in film culture, was unprecedented. Never before had anybody seen such harsh realism on the screen, such large-scale presentation of nature, such brutally and convincingly outlined conflicts between simple people with whom all spectators could identify. Compared with the cosmopolitan, escapist Danish or Italian films of the day, Swedish film art was bringing a fresh wind of truth molded into impeccable artistic shape.

The Outlaw and His Wife clearly revealed the trait that was to become the dominant characteristic of all Scandinavian art, and not the cinema only. This was the need for redemption through nature as reflected in Northern, Protestant mentality, the need for purification of the soul through the intermediary of such natural phenomena as snow or fire.

ABOVE: At the wealthy farm of Halla. BELOW: Berg-Ejvind, the Lapland settler, in happy coexistence with nature.

ABOVE: A fight for life in the wilderness. BELOW: The last shelter.

ABOVE: A winter blizzard is coming. BELOW: United by mutual love.

SIR ARNE'S TREASURE

(Swedish title: "Herr Arnes pengar" [literally, "Sir Arne's Money"].)

Produced 1919 by AB Svenska Biografteatern. Released September 22, 1919.

Director: Mauritz Stiller. Screenplay (based on the story by Selma Lagerlöf: Gustaf Molander and Mauritz Stiller. Camera: Julius Jaenzon. Art Director: Harry Dahlström.

CAST: Richard Lund (*Sir Archie*); Eric Stocklassa (*Sir Filip*); Bror Berger (*Sir Donald*); Hjalmar Selander (*Herr Arne*); Concordia Selander (*his wife*); Mary Johnson (*Elsalill*); Wanda Rothgardt (*Berghild*); Axel Nilsson (*Torarin*); Jenny Öhrström-Ebbesen (*his mother*); Gustav Aronson (*skipper*); Stina Berg (*hostess at the liquor establishment*); Gösta Gustafsson (*vicar*).

SYNOPSIS & COMMENTARY: While Sjöström was clearing the way for the new Swedish style in film, his friendly rival Mauritz Stiller was still considering the choice of a creative trend suitable for him. During the triumphal period of Sjöström's *Terje Vigen* and *The Outlaw and His Wife*, Stiller was polishing his comedy style (incidentally, in Stiller's two Thomas Graal pictures it was Sjöström who was cast in the title role). Stiller's first attempt to abandon the drawing-room scenery for the outdoors was his 1918 film version of a popular Finnish novel by Johannes Linnakoski that was to be adapted for the screen many times in the future: *Song of the Scarlet Flower* (Sången om den eldröda blomman). The story, intermittently dramatic and lyrical, develops in an environment of peasants and craftsmen, and in Stiller's version had the healthy openness of a production shot on location, free of all restrictions imposed by studio sets. But it was not until *Sir Arne's Treasure*, based on a Selma Lagerlöf story, that Stiller made a major new contribution to the achievements of the Swedish film school. According to Svenska's initial plans, Sjöström, the acknowledged Lagerlöf expert, was supposed to direct the film, but at the last moment he ceded the subject to Stiller.

The story is set late in the sixteenth century when the Scottish mercenary guards of King Johan III Vasa rioted. Three Scottish officers, arrested upon suppression of the riot, escape from prison. Exhausted and desperate, ready for anything that will help them get back to their native land, they arrive at the parish where Sir Arne is the most substantial resident. They murder all the population there and escape carrying a case full of treasure to the west-coast port of Marstrand. The only person spared in the shambles is Elsalill, Arne's foster daughter, who had taken shelter at a fishmonger's. Spring comes, but the sea is still icebound. One of the Scottish officers, Sir Archie, meets Elsalill and they fall in love, the girl not recognizing the murderers of her foster parents. But in her sleep she sees the ghost of Berghild, her foster sister: it is a presentiment of the grisly truth soon to be revealed. The girl indicates the murderers to the royal guard but, wishing at the last moment to save the man she loves, she dies pierced by a spear. A procession of mourning women carries her body across the ice-covered bay. Sir Archie and his comrades are captured.

Stiller and his scriptwriter Molander simplified the meandering plot of the story, making the narration more consistent and building up tension in a logical way justified by the development of events. With his perfect management of actors, Stiller succeeded in giving an impressive presentation of the psychologically complex relationship of the two lovers, depicting the intensity of a situation that forces the heroine to make a tragic choice. Mary Johnson, though very young, proved to be, as the major French film critic Louis Delluc put it, "the true gem of this film." As director, Stiller demonstrated a masterly feeling for image. In the famous final scene, a geometrically arranged line of dark figures on the white plane of snow and ice is one of the greatest accomplishments of silent cinema. It was repeated in a number of variations by such other directors as Erwin Piscator—in *The Revolt of the Fishermen* (Vosstanije rybakov), 1934—and Sergei Eisenstein—in *Ivan the Terrible* (Ivan Groznyi), 1945.

ABOVE: The Scottish mercenaries escape with Sir Arne's treasure. BELOW: In a dream, Elsalill follows her dead foster sister.

ABOVE: Elsalill just before hearing the truth about the murderers of her family. BELOW: She informs the guards of the murderers' whereabouts.

ABOVE: Elsalill warns Sir Archie about the guards. BELOW: Elsalill's body carried across the ice-covered bay of Marstrand.

EROTIKON

(Swedish Title: "Erotikon.")

Produced 1920 by AB Svensk Filmindustri. Released November 8, 1920.

Director: Mauritz Stiller. Screenplay (based on the play *A kék róka* [The Blue Fox] by Ferenc Herczeg): Mauritz Stiller. Camera: Henrik Jaenzon. Art Director: Axel Esbensen.

CAST: Anders de Wahl (*Lev Charpentier, an entomology professor*); Tora Teje (*Irene, his wife*); Karin Molander (*Marthe, his niece*); Elin Lagergren (*Irene's mother*); Lars Hanson (*Preben Wells, a sculptor*); Vilhelm Bryde (*Baron Felix*); Bell Hedqvist (*his girl friend*); Torsten Hammarén (*Sidonius, a professor*); Vilhelm Berntsson (*Jean, a butler*); Stina Berg (*a faithful old servant*); John Lindlöf (*Preben's friend*); Greta Lindgren (*Preben's model*); Curt Wallin (*a fur dealer*); Gucken Cederborg (*a cook*); Tora Wibergh (*Jenny, a housemaid*); Carina Ari (*Schaname, in the ballet*); Martin Oscár (*the Shah, in the ballet*).

SYNOPSIS & COMMENTARY: *Erotikon* is generally considered as the peak achievement of the comedy trend in Stiller's work. Based on a Hungarian play and essentially an intimate comedy of manners, *Erotikon* was produced vigorously and lavishly in hopes of achieving an international box-office success. The film contained views shot from an airplane—a rarity at that time—and the performance of the Stockholm Opera ballet to specially composed music was meant to be the chief attraction of the show.

Irene is the wife of Professor Charpentier, an entomologist preoccupied with his bugs. Neglected by her husband, she is flirting with several men. One of them, Baron Felix, takes her for an airplane spin. Their plane flies over the studio of Preben, a young sculptor and the best friend of the Charpentiers. Preben jealously watches their passage through the air. Meanwhile Marthe, the professor's niece, who pretends that entomology is her hobby and who is dedicatedly taking care of the Charpentier household, is gradually entrapping her uncle romantically. All of them visit the Opera to see the ballet *Schaname*. Its plot—with the Shah, his favorite slave and the Shah's friend—suddenly gives reality to the secret thoughts of Irene and Preben. Still jealous of Baron Felix, Preben finds that he cannot remain at the Opera. Irene and Preben meet next day and Preben demands an explanation. Irene defies him and the enamored sculptor tries to arrange a duel between the Professor and Baron Felix, which is luckily prevented by Marthe, the only one who keeps a cool head on her shoulders. The denouement is fortunate for everybody involved: Irene gets a divorce, while Marthe gets the Professor and can at last stop pretending she is the humble homebody.

Spiciness, libertinism and even a touch of cynicism in the situations entertained and shocked the Swedish public. The picture ran in a first-run theater for three weeks, a record at that time. The director had gathered a company of excellent actors with Anders de Wahl making his screen debut and the charming Tora Teje as the feminine lead. Stiller took full advantage of his extensive stage experience, dazzling the audience with the splendor of the sets, which he designed himself, and with the fabulous clothing worn by the leading lady. He wanted to entertain and to charm, and he did.

Erotikon was perhaps even a greater hit outside of Sweden, especially in Germany where enthusiastic opinions about Stiller's film were voiced by such theater people as Max Reinhardt and such film people as Dimitri Buchowetzki. Ernst Lubitsch used *Erotikon* as a source of inspiration for his cycle of sophisticated comedies made in Hollywood during the Twenties and Thirties. The style had late repercussions in films by Billy Wilder, Richard Quine and Blake Edwards, and even Jean Renoir admitted its impact on him when making *The Rules of the Game* (La règle du jeu). The Swedish cinema, however, did not continue in this style, but remained faithful to its own tradition of dramatic pictures linked with nature and folklore. Four years later Stiller moved to Hollywood and tried rather unsuccessfully to repeat the *Erotikon* formula in parts of *Hotel Imperial*, which starred Pola Negri. It was not until the Sixties that Swedish critics found a touch of Stiller's former refinement in some of Bergman's comedies, and it was to Stiller that Jörn Donner dedicated his *To Love* (Att älska), 1964.

Irene, the neglected wife of Professor Charpentier (ABOVE) . . . counts among her admirers Baron Felix, who takes her on a spin in a plane (BELOW).

ABOVE: Meanwhile Martha, the professor's niece, pretends to be interested only in entomology. BELOW: Another, strong rival for Irene's heart is Preben, the sculptor.

The professor finally falls into his niece's trap (ABOVE), divorces his wife and . . . is congratulated by her on the phone (BELOW).

THE PHANTOM CARRIAGE

(Swedish title: "Körkarlen" [literally, "The Coachman"]. Original U.S. distribution title: "The Stroke of Midnight." Original British distribution title: "Thy Soul Shall Bear Witness.")

Produced 1920 by AB Svensk Filmindustri. Released January 1, 1921.

Director: Victor Sjöström. Screenplay (based on the novel by Selma Lagerlöf): Victor Sjöström. Camera: Julius Jaenzon. Art Directors: Axel Esbensen, Alexander Bakó.

CAST: Victor Sjöström (*David Holm*); Hilda Borgström (*his wife*); Tore Svennberg (*Georges*); Astrid Holm (*Sister Edit*); Lisa Lundholm (*Sister Maria*); Tor Weijden (*Gustafsson*); Concordia Selander (*Edit's mother*); Einar Axelsson (*David's brother*); Nils Aréhn (*prison clergyman*); Simon Lindstrand & Nils Elffors (*David's buddies in the cemetery*); Olof Ås (*the driver*); Algot Gunnarsson (*a worker*); Hildur Lithman (*a worker's wife*); John Ekman (*police officer*); Josua Bengtsson (*card player*); Emmy Albiin (*consumptive woman*); Mona Geijer-Falkner (*restaurant waitress*).

SYNOPSIS & COMMENTARY: *The Phantom Carriage* was hailed as a masterpiece on its first appearance, but the passage of time deprived it of much of the surprise effect that its technical novelties had had on its early audiences. Nevertheless, the image of the ghost carriage moving over the waves of the sea and along the far line of the horizon, seemingly immaterial thanks to double (in some scenes even triple) exposure in the masterly camera work of Julius Jaenzon, affects our imagination even today. None of the subsequent screen versions of Selma Lagerlöf's novel has reached the power of expression of this one. Sjöström's film is not as inventive in its psychological stratum but his social and moralizing interests are curiously interwoven with his personal experiences. Both the presence of actress Hilda Borgström and the name of the character she is playing hark back to another movie, *Ingeborg Holm*, which film historian Bengt Idestam-Almquist presumes was Sjöström's tribute to his own mother. Seen in the same personal way, *The Phantom Carriage* is Sjöström coming to terms with his own father. Sjöström himself plays David Holm with surprising realism, using no make-up. Through the character he voices his protest against moral degradation as well as the necessity of subordinating life to the strict rules proclaimed by Selma Lagerlöf.

David Holm is a drunkard. It was his pal Georges who led him into this addiction. Holm goes to prison leaving his family reduced to destitution. When released, he discovers that his wife and children have left him, but there is no effort on his part to change his way of life for their sake. He keeps staggering from one saloon to another, spending his nights in flophouses. Sister Edit of the Salvation Army fights for his reformation, which to her means the salvation of his soul. On New Year's Eve David does meet his family but the encounter ends in an argument so violent that his wife decides to poison herself and the children. Holm is awaiting the arrival of the New Year at the cemetery where he tells his drinking companions the legend of the Coachman of Death. They drink and a fight ensues; a painful blow knocks Holm unconscious. That is when the ghost carriage comes to claim him, driven by Georges, who had died a year earlier. Holm is overwhelmed by fear and repentance. Upon regaining consciousness he hurries to his wife and arrives just in time to save her and the children from death. Sister Edit dies happy because she has been able to save a human soul.

The story is told in an intricate system of flashbacks: time stops prior to the start of a new annual cycle; the future and the past acquire the same reality. Sjöström applied a variety of technical means (special lighting and printing) to make clear the differences between current event and flashback, reality and dream, consciousness and sleep, the indicative and conditional moods. These differences are additionally emphasized by the sharp contrast between the violence of the naturalistic scenes and the mysticism of the spiritual scenes—a mysticism of both Protestant and folk origin.

The picture had great impact on the style of poetical films of later years, including Jean Cocteau's *The Blood of a Poet* (Le Sang d'un Poète). Its classic pictorial beauty, earnestness and mastery of narrative make *The Phantom Carriage* one of the most outstanding works of the silent cinema, alongside *The Gold Rush* and *The Battleship Potemkin* (Bronenosets Potyomkin).

ABOVE: Holm awaits the arrival of the New Year in the cemetery with his buddies. BELOW: The drunken Holm mocking the Salvation Army ceremony.

ABOVE: The ghost carriage comes to get Holm. BELOW: Holm's soul leaves his body.

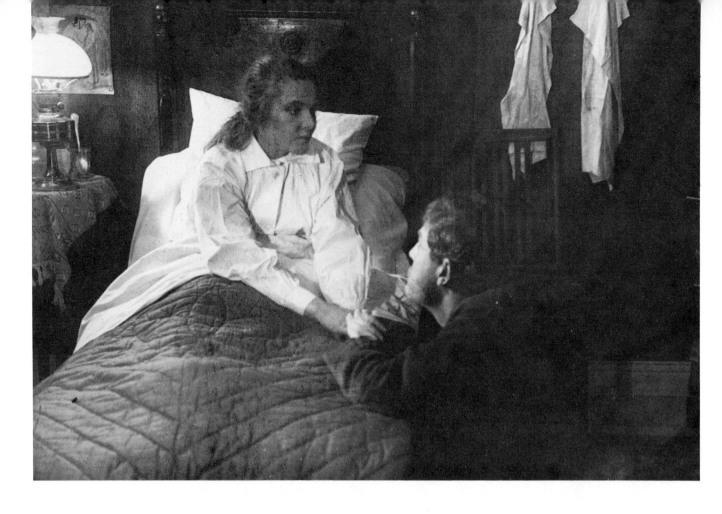

ABOVE: Sister Edit on her deathbed. BELOW: Holm entering his home before the final reconciliation.

THE ATONEMENT OF GÖSTA BERLING

(Swedish title: "Gösta Berlings saga." Alternate English-language titles replace "Atonement" by "Story," "Legend" or "Saga.")

Produced 1924 by AB Svensk Filmindustri. Released in two parts on March 10 and 17, 1924.

Director: Mauritz Stiller. Screenplay (based on the novel by Selma Lagerlöf): Mauritz Stiller, Ragnar Hyltén-Cavallius. Camera: Julius Jaenzon. Art Directors: Ragnar Brattén, Vilhelm Bryde.

CAST: Lars Hanson (*Gösta Berling*); Gerda Lundequist (*Margareta Samzelius*); Hilda Forsslund (*her mother*); Otto Elg-Lundberg (*Major Samzelius*); Sixten Malmerfeldt (*Melchior Sinclaire*); Karin Swanström (*Gustafva, his wife*); Jenny Hasselqvist (*Marianne, their daughter*); Ellen Cederström (*Countess Märtha Dohna*); Torsten Hammarén (*Count Henrik Dohna, her son*); Greta Garbo (*Elisabeth Dohna, his wife*); Mona Mårtenson (*Countess Ebba Dohna, his sister*); Sven Scholander (*Sintram*). THE "CAVALIERS" AT EKEBY: Svend Kornbeck (*Christian Bergh, former captain*); Hugo Rönnblad (*Beerencreutz*); Knut Lambert (*Rutger von Örneclou*); Oscar Bergström (*Master Julius*); Jules Gaston-Portefaix (*Anders Fuchs, former major*); Albert Ståhl (*Uncle Eberhard*); Anton de Verdier (*Cousin Kristoffer*); Axel Jacobsson (*Lilliencrona*); Jan de Meyere (*Löwenborg*); Edmund Hohndorf (*Kevenhüller*); Theodor Buch (*Ruster*); Birger Lyne (*a "cavalier"*).

SYNOPSIS & COMMENTARY: Though the film version of *Sir Arne's Treasure* was a success, Selma Lagerlöf was unhappy with the deviations from her original novel that Mauritz Stiller had introduced. Her conflict with the director was aggravated after the premiere of *The Blizzard* (Gunnar Hedes saga; British release title, *The Judgement*) in 1922. Stiller made free use of the text, constructing a self-standing work; he canceled episodes, added some of his own and—what was most important —changed the locales the plot developed in. The writer, indignant, stated she would never again allow such use to be made of any of her works. But Magnusson, the head of SF, thought that only Stiller was able to direct the screen version of her particularly famous first novel, *Gösta Berlings saga* (1891). As a result of extreme diplomacy on Stiller's part, Selma Lagerlöf finally assented, but not before giving the screenplay a thorough examination. Despite the director's written pledge to be faithful to this agreed-on version, the writer did protest again when the two parts of the film were released.

The changes proved to have been a necessity for the picture, allowing it to embrace a wealth of genre scenes illustrative of Värmland aristocratic life at the turn of the nineteenth century. Stiller altered the chronological order of the narration. It is difficult today to reproduce the construction of the original film because a few years after its first release the two parts were combined into one, after being reedited and abridged. Even in this shortened version, however, its epic vigor and boldness of production are still evident.

The title character, Gösta Berling, an unfrocked pastor, is hired as tutor to Ebba Dohna, a young lady of the nobility. The girl falls in love with him, as does Elisabeth, the beauty whom the landowner Henrik had brought from Italy, unaware of the fact that their marriage was technically illegal. When Gösta has to leave the Dohna household, he finds shelter at Ekeby Castle, where he takes up an idle, carousing life as one of the many "cavaliers"—impoverished scions of the nobility living as guests of Margareta, Major Samzelius' wife. Gösta falls in love with Marianne Sinclaire, who resides in the neighborhood. When her father, indignant, expels her from the house, Gösta takes her to Ekeby with him. Soon afterward she is stricken by smallpox and loses her good looks. In the meantime Lady Margareta, having quarreled with her mother and her husband, departs from the castle. The "cavaliers" take over, but their licentious way of life causes a peasants' mutiny. An unknown arsonist sets fire to the castle. Gösta saves Marianne from the flames. She is now ready to go back to her parents. When Gösta sees Elisabeth again, he has changed; he decides to settle down. Lady Margareta gives her blessing to his marriage with Elisabeth and entrusts the reconstruction of the castle to him.

During the difficult production period, Stiller was frequently carried away by his creative temperament and overexpanded the spectacular scenes. The most interesting of these are the fire in the castle and the frantic sleigh ride over an icebound lake with a pack of wolves in pursuit. The perfectly used locations are somewhat inconsistent with the scenes shot at the studio though Stiller was able to extract even from his interiors a plastic beauty reminiscent of Vermeer's paintings. The film is not as uniform in style as *Sir Arne's Treasure* or the same director's high-society comedies, but it is still the work of a master and was acclaimed in Sweden and abroad. Only a few months after the premiere, Stiller signed his Hollywood contract. His example was soon followed by the nineteen-year-old actress who had been cast as Elisabeth. She was Greta-Lovisa Gustafsson, who appeared in movies as Greta Garbo.

ABOVE: The sermon of the pastor, who is soon to be dismissed from his office. BELOW: Count Henrik Dohna comes home with his Italian wife Elisabeth.

ABOVE: Gösta as tutor to Ebba Dohna. BELOW: Gösta finds shelter at Ekeby Castle, among other "cavaliers."

ABOVE: Major Samzelius exiles his wife from Ekeby. BELOW: Gösta and Elisabeth Dohna decide to settle down together.

CHARLES XII

(Swedish title: "Karl XII.")

Produced 1925 by Historisk Film & Herman Rasch. Released in two parts on February 2 and November 16, 1925.

Director: John W. Brunius. Screenplay: Hjalmar Bergman, Ivar Johansson. Camera: Hugo Edlund. Art Directors: Vilhelm Bryde, Allan Egnell. Music: Otto Trobäck.

CAST: Gösta Ekman (*Karl XII*); Bengt Djurberg (*Sven Björnberg*); Augusta Lindberg (*Kerstin Ulfclou at Berga*); Mona Mårtenson (*Anna Ulfclou*); Harry Roeck Hansen (*Erik Ulfclou*); Axel Lagerberg (*Johan Ulfclou*); Paul Seelig (*Bengt Ulfclou*); Palle Brunius (*Lasse Ulfclou*); Tyra Dörum (*Kajsa, maid at Berga*); Nicolai de Seversky (*Czar Peter I*); Pauline Brunius (*Aurora Königsmarck*); Tor Weijden (*August the Strong*); Einar Fröberg (*Fredrik IV of Denmark*); Ragnar Billberg (*Hans Küsel*); Nika de Seversky (*Ayscha*); Mignon Georgian (*her sister, the Sultan's favorite wife*); Rudolf Wendbladh (*the Sultan*); Josef Fischer (*the Grand Vizir*); Alf Lindgren (*Alexej, a Russian prince*); Birger Lyne (*Sachar, the Czar's servant*); Hugo Björne (*Prince Fredrik of Holstein-Gottorp*); Gustaf Ranft (*Hans Wachtmeister, a general*); Gösta Ericsson (*Prince Max of Württemberg*); Paul Lane (*Poniatowski*); Thor Modéen (*von Görtz*); Sven Bergvall (*Ivan Mazepa*); Gustaf Runsten (*Kristoffer Polhem*); Gabriel Alw (*Emanuel Swedenborg*); Georg Funkquist (*Düring, a lieutenant-colonel*); Märta Ekström (*Katarina, the Czar's wife*).

SYNOPSIS & COMMENTARY: An ambitious effort to extend the period of greatness in Swedish films was made by industry tycoon Herman Rasch, who hired John Brunius, veteran of Skandia's pioneering days, to direct a monumental two-part historical drama on Charles XII. The film crew was granted nearly unlimited resources. Accurate historical research was undertaken and Rasch himself traveled all along the route Charles XII had followed when returning to Sweden after his defeat at Poltava in 1709. Many scenes were shot at the very sites where they had taken place. A choice group of actors was cast in the picture, with Gösta Ekman in the lead. The course of these historical events, preserved in the Swedish nation's collective memory, was reproduced in an imaginatively written screenplay by renowned author Hjalmar Bergman.

When Charles XII came to the throne in 1697 he was only fifteen. Already inheritor of an enormous kingdom, three years later he began a series of armed operations in the Baltic Sea basin. The film tells of the King's expeditions against the Danes, Russians, Saxons and Poles, of his victory at Narva and of his final confrontation with Russia, ended by the disastrous defeat at Poltava. Charles XII had to withdraw to Turkey with what was left of his troops and tried to involve that nation in a war against the Russians. But meanwhile, in an impoverished Sweden, strong pacifist trends began to threaten his reign. He left Turkey and traveled post-haste to the port of Stralsund, making 2000 kilometers in fourteen days. He failed in his attempts to sign a separate treaty either with England as ally against Russia or with Russia as ally against England. To make up for Sweden's losses of territory, he invaded neighboring Norway. While besieging Fredrikssten fortress in that country in 1718, he was killed by a stray bullet.

The second line of action follows the story of the noble family Ulfclou, owner of the Berga estate. The young king Karl XII pays a visit to them while the youngest son, Lasse, is out alone on a bear hunt. Eventually the King and his men save Lasse's life when he is in trouble, wounded by the raging bear. Lasse's sister Anna is in love with one of the King's knights, Sven Björnberg, while Lady Kerstin Ulfclou prefers another candidate for son-in-law, Hans Küsel. Sven and Anna marry in a hasty wartime ceremony, and they both leave Berga for the front. After some time Lasse and the old servant Kajsa follow them. During the campaign in Russia and Poland Sven is caught and tortured by the Russian troops, while Anna returns alone to Berga. During the following battles against the Russians, and especially after the Poltava disaster and during the King's sojourn in Turkey, Lasse takes part in an intrigue with a beautiful Turkish woman, Ayscha. Together they visit the Sultan's court at Constantinople in order to defend the King against the intrigues of the Grand Vizir. After his return to Sweden, the King once again saves Lasse's life during the campaign in Norway. He also shows great generosity toward the Ulfclou family by annulling their tax obligations to the state.

Brunius did not overcome the danger of excessive trappings. The spectacular and vigorous battle scenes are not matched by the more intimate sequences, which are conventional scenes of court intrigue. The film is impressive in size, but essentially illustrative and lifeless. In Sweden it was a great success, but never recouped its production expenses of about a million kroner. This made *Charles XII* the second most expensive Swedish film up to that time after Christensen's *Witchcraft Through the Ages* (Häxan).

In the next few years Rasch and Brunius made two more films based on history. But neither *Fänrik Ståls sägner* (The Legends of Ensign Stål) of 1926, based on poems by Johan Ludvig Runeberg, nor *Gustav Vasa* of 1928 was able to bring back the old glamor to Swedish films or to overcome their provincial isolation.

ABOVE: The action at Bender: Karl XII and his soldiers attacked by the Turks. BELOW: Karl is killed by a stray bullet during the siege of Fredrikssten.

ONE NIGHT

(Swedish title: "En natt.")

Produced 1931 by AB Svensk Filmindustri. Released September 14, 1931.

Director: Gustaf Molander. Screenplay: Ragnar Hyltén-Cavallius. Camera: Åke Dahlqvist. Art Director: Arne Åkermark. Music: Jules Sylvain, Peter Lebedjeff, Jean Sibelius.

CAST: Gerda Lundequist (*Lady Beckius*); Uno Henning (*Wilhelm, her son*); Björn Berglund (*Armas, her son*); Ingert Bjuggren (*Marja*); Karin Swanström (*Minka*); Sture Lagerwall (*Nikku*); Carl Ström (*Captain Karr*); Mathey Schischkin & Tom Walter (*Russian soldiers*); Gösta Kjellertz (*standard-bearer*); Nils Lundell (*Red soldier on train*); Emil Fjellström (*White officer*); Carl Winsberg (*a servant*).

SYNOPSIS & COMMENTARY: The setting is Finnish Karelia in 1918, with civil war ravaging the country. The noble Beckius family is torn by conflicting loyalties, honor versus social radicalism, tradition versus riot. Armas, the family's younger son, is disloyal to the duties of his class: he loves Marja, a simple Russian girl, and joins the workers' reinforcement troops arriving from revolutionary Russia. His mother, a colonel's wife, disowns him. Caught by the Whites and sentenced to be executed at dawn, Armas is paroled for the night by his older brother, a captain in the White army. Though Marja is reluctant to let Armas return to certain death, Armas fights his way through the front lines. Fatally wounded, he reports at the appointed site. On hearing the news, his mother breathes with relief: the honor of the family is saved.

This early sound film of Molander's, drastically different from the later comedies and salon dramas characteristic of his output, lack uniformity, is poorly motivated psychologically and takes no sides in the conflict. The fact that it was acknowledged as the artistically most outstanding Swedish picture of the Thirties (which Jean Béranger called "the years of lethargy") is due to its bold experimental approach on the formal side.

Scriptwriter Hyltén-Cavallius and director Gustaf Molander, both representatives of the generation that had created the Swedish school of the silent period, found in 23-year-old Gösta Hellström—a film zealot and critic who was debuting as assistant director—a spirit of artistic renovation that under more favorable circumstances might have led the Swedish cinema toward new creative areas. Two years earlier Hellström had visited the Soviet Union, met Eisenstein and Pudovkin and studied their works thoroughly. In *One Night* the impact of the dynamic Soviet style of editing is evident. Present to a lesser extent is the creative approach to nature typical of the older Swedish school as well as an expressionism strongly reminiscent of certain scenes in Ermler's *Fragment of an Empire* (Oblomok imperii) of 1927.

The appearance of *One Night*—along with Alf Sjöberg's directorial debut *The Strongest* (Den starkaste), 1929—was the first, still modest announcement of the renewal that the Swedish film would not really enjoy until the Forties. Though it harked back to the esthetics of the silent masterpieces, it was ahead of its time by Swedish standards. For SF, the production firm, *One Night* was also a frightening example of what it meant to "disregard the public's taste": the film was a disastrous box-office flop. It did not create any school, nor did it have any artistic follow-ups.

The hopes for Gösta Hellström's further progress also failed to materialize. He died of tuberculosis a year later, having made only two more films, of which one was the experimental short *Tango*.

ABOVE: Armas returns home with the revolutionary troops. BELOW: He is sentenced to death.

Paroled for the night (ABOVE) . . . he visits his girl, Marja (BELOW).

Marja tries to save Armas against his will (ABOVE) . . . but an old servant, Minka, lets him out (BELOW).

KARL FREDRIK REIGNS

(Swedish title: "Karl Fredrik regerar.")

Produced 1934 by AB Svensk Filmindustri. Released March 3, 1934.

Director: Gustaf Edgren. Screenplay: Oscar Rydqvist. Camera: Åke Dahlqvist, Martin Bodin. Art Director: Arne Åkermark. Music: Eric Bengtsson; Jacques Offenbach, Pierre Degeyter, Edvard Grieg, Otto Lindblad. Editor: Rolf Husberg.

CAST: Hugo Björne (*Major Carl Lindberg, landowner*); Pauline Brunius *(his wife)*; Björn Berglund (*Olof, their son*); Sigurd Wallén (*Karl Fredrik Pettersson*); Dora Söderberg (*Maja, his wife*); Gull-Maj Norin (*Lena, their daughter*); Dagmar Ebbesen *(Augusta, their housekeeper)*; Carl Ström (*Eriksson, an administrator*); Gertrud Pålsson-Wettergren & Helga Görlin (*opera soloists*); Eric Abrahamsson (*Öberg, a newspaper editor*); Charlie Almlöf (*a propagandist*); Sigge Fürst (*Bergdahl, an articled clerk*); Henning Ohlson (*Bogren, a cotter*); Britt-Lis Edgren (*Lena as a child*); Bengt Edgren (*Olof as a child*); Emil Fjellström & Holger Löwenadler (*cotters*); John Melin(*Communist speaker at election campaign*); Eric Gustafson (*Nazi speaker at election campaign*); Olof Sandborg (*Conservative speaker at election campaign*); Dagmar Olsson (*coffeehouse waitress*); Tom Walter (*land worker*); Eric Dahlström (*clerk at the department of agriculture*); Kotti Chave (*porter at the department of agriculture*); Nils Jacobson (*night editor*); Georg Fernquist (*Olsson, a servant*); Gunnar Skoglund (*a man by the boat*); Hugo Tranberg (*stationmaster*); Gustaf Edgren (*his pal*); Tor Borong (*an aggressive cotter*).

SYNOPSIS & COMMENTARY: The Depression years, with their strikes, demonstrations, unemployment and eventually the Social Democrat regime in Sweden, created a climate favoring socially committed films. Even though the majority of pictures made were still in the "bush" or "Pilsner film" folk-show class, a small but outstanding group of *films engagés* was produced. Some were semiamateur with a nonprofessional cast; others were made with money from unions or from the Social Democrat party as propaganda in the election campaign. Mats A. Stenström's *The Outcasts* (De utstötta) of 1931, for instance, imitated the atmosphere of such German "Zille films" as *Mother Krausen's Journey to Happiness* (Mutter Krausens Fahrt ins Glück) or *Berlin-Alexanderplatz*. There also were some proletarian motifs in *Steel*

(Stål), 1939, by Per Lindberg, and *Conflict* (Konflikt), 1937, by Per Axel Brenner.

The most interesting example of a picture reflecting social changes in the Sweden of the early Thirties was *Karl Fredrik Reigns* by Gustaf Edgren, who had been known earlier as a director of trite comedies starring Fridolf Rhudin. John Sanden, publicist and Social Democrat deputy to Parliament, was the co-author of the original story. The hero combined characteristics of several popular Social Democrat politicians including Premier Per Albin Hansson, and in one of the minor roles, that of a speaker at a workers' rally, posterity recognized Gunnar Sträng, later to be finance minister in the Social Democrat government.

The prologue tells of the period shortly before World War I. The merciless administrator of Major Lindberg's estate drives Karl Fredrik Pettersson, a mutinous stable hand, away from the farm. As he departs by horse and wagon with the whole family and their wretched belongings, the landowner's spoiled little son throws stones at Lena, Pettersson's daughter, a girl of his own age. Years pass. Major Lindberg dies and so does Maja, Karl Fredrik's wife. Lena becomes a journalist at the workers' daily newspaper. One day, the Petterssons, father and daughter, together with their housekeeper, Augusta, take a spin in a motorboat on a lake and trespass on private property. In that way Lena gets acquainted with Olof, a young violinist, who happens to be Mrs. Lindberg's son. They fall in love, despite Mrs. Lindberg's strong opposition to her son's intended misalliance. Eventually she is reconciled to the situation, because in the meantime Karl Fredrik has become minister of agriculture in the Social Democrat government and can save the Lindbergs' estate from bankruptcy by arranging a state loan. At the same time he legislates improvements in the farm laborers' working conditions.

This symbolical gesture of class reconciliation anticipated by four years the historical Saltsjöbaden resolutions, which were of decisive impact on the social development of modern Sweden.

Swedish films of the Thirties, even in their most mature and ambitious aspects, drew very little inspiration from worthwhile literature, in contrast to the silent period. The social protest represented by the writings of the so-called Farmhand School (Ivar Lo-Johansson, Jan Fridegård and Harry Martinson) were not to be reflected in films until the late Forties.

ABOVE: Karl Fredrik Pettersson disseminates socialist propaganda at a meeting of farm workers. BELOW: The Petterssons are forced to depart from the Lindberg estate.

ABOVE: After the Petterssons trespass on private property, Lena meets Olof Lindberg. BELOW: Lena and Olof fall in love.

ABOVE: Mrs. Lindberg has strong doubts about her son's marriage plans. BELOW: But Karl Frederik Pettersson, who is now minister of agriculture in a Social Democrat government, solves the financial problems of her estate.

INTERMEZZO

(Swedish title: "Intermezzo.")

Produced 1936 by AB Svensk Filmindustri. Released November 16, 1936.

Director: Gustaf Molander. Screenplay: Gustaf Molander, Gösta Stevens. Camera: Åke Dahlqvist. Art Director: Arne Åkermark. Music: Heinz Provost; J. S. Bach, Christian Sinding, Franz Schubert, Fryderyk Chopin, Hilding Rosenberg, Jules Buisson, Peter Tchaikovsky. Editor: Oscar Rosander.

CAST: Gösta Ekman (*Holger Brandt*); Inga Tidblad (*Margit, his wife*); Ingrid Bergman (*Anita Hoffman*); Hasse Ekman (*Åke, Brandt's son*); Britt Hagman (*Ann-Marie, Brandt's daughter*); Erik "Bullen" Berglund (*Charles Möller, an impresario*); Hugo Björne (*Thomas Stenborg*); Emma Meissner (*Greta, his wife*); Ruth Weijden (*Mrs. Lindberg*); Anders Henrikson (*an unknown seaman*); Margareta Orth (*Marie*); George Fant & Folke Helleberg (*two young men*); Minnan Bolander (*Emma, a housemaid*); Carl Ström (*a man*).

SYNOPSIS & COMMENTARY: In the Italian "white telephone" filmmaking of the Thirties, the directors who attempted to cover the emptiness of their work with elegance of craftsmanship were called "calligraphers." Sweden's leading, if not only, "calligrapher" was Gustaf Molander. Among his films one can find a few light comedies, but of the twenty-three films he made during the first decade of sound, most were society dramas, set for the most part in the higher social strata. The stereotyped nature of the scripts, the sameness of the situations, usually variations on the Cinderella story, the sense of claustrophobia caused by the confining studio sets with their numerous props and decorations intended to represent "high life," were compensated for by Molander with a refined directorial culture, a highly developed art of cooperation with a team of good leading players and a smoothness of directorial design. His films might have been unimportant entertainment, but never boring.

Along with the titular aristocracy, an inheritance from the early silent films with their "counts and barons"; along with the aristocracy of wealth—bankers and leaders of the growing industries —Molander also showed in his films the aristocracy of spirit: outstanding scientists (such as Nobel Prize winner Professor Swedenhielm in a movie version of Hjalmar Bergman's drama *Swedenhielms*) and artists (such as Professor Brandt, the violinist in *Intermezzo*). In both films the main parts were played by Gösta Ekman and a promising young actress, Ingrid Bergman.

Brandt is a virtuoso who gives little thought to his loyal and silently tormented wife Margit. His friend and accompanist Thomas Stenborg is unable to join him on his forthcoming world tour. Brandt finds a new accompanist, the young pianist Anita Hoffman who has been teaching his daughter Ann-Marie. Anita gradually becomes important in his life as a new inspiration, a renaissance of feelings. Margit Brandt fears this situation more than she fears her husband's long trips abroad, more than she fears her own loneliness. Anonymous letters and rumors force Anita to withdraw from the partnership. She tries to take the train to Denmark, but Brandt succeeds in stopping her. Brandt and Anita set out on an idyllic concert tour together. Anita is the first to be aware not only that they were first joined together by a musical piece called "Intermezzo," but also that their love was only an intermezzo in Brandt's well-structured life. When Brandt returns to Stockholm, his little daughter has an accident. In the hospital corridor, as the message arrives that she is out of danger, Brandt comes to terms with his wife.

Intermezzo, a huge box-office and critical success of the late Thirties, has lost most of its merit today. A viewing of it is also somewhat destructive of the former reputation of its star, Gösta Ekman. Actually, he never totally rid himself of an irritating stage technique. Probably his most coherent and well worked-out film performance was in a less well-known picture directed by Lorens Marmstedt, *Perhaps a Poet?* (Kanske en diktare?), 1933. In his other, more important and far more famous parts, Ekman is devastatingly old-fashioned; his feelings are painted on his face in a literary manner, depriving the spectator of the possibility for choice or error. *Intermezzo* was, on the other hand, a beginning of the magnificent career of Ingrid Bergman. Her role in this film made her known to Hollywood talent scouts and within three years she made her debut in the United States in a remake of the same film. The Hollywood engagement was hardly a temptation for Gustaf Molander and the film was directed by Gregory Ratoff.

Intermezzo was not the very best film directed by Molander during the Thirties. *Swedenhielms*, 1935, is more interesting for its depiction of a certain social stratum, and *A Woman's Face* (En kvinnas ansikte), 1938, is psychologically more daring and violent and in some parts more refined. But *Intermezzo* still remains one of the best examples of a certain mentality, typical of its time and influence on film audiences and filmmakers alike.

ABOVE: The violin virtuoso Holger Brandt returns from a concert tour. BELOW: Brandt falls in love with the young pianist Anita Hoffman.

ABOVE: Holger and Anita together on their foreign tour. BELOW: Brandt's wife and daughter at home.

ABOVE: Young Åke Brandt criticizes his father's behavior. BELOW: Brandt returns to his family obligations.

LIFE AT STAKE

(Swedish title: "Med livet som insats.")

Produced 1939 by AB Artist Film. Released January 1, 1940.

Director: Alf Sjöberg. Screenplay (based on the short story by Runar Schildt): Theodor Berthels, Alf Sjöberg, Christen Jul. Camera: Harald Berglund. Art Director: Max Linder. Music: Moses Pergament.

CAST: Aino Taube (*Wanda*); Åke Ohberg (*John*); Anders Henrikson (*Max*); Holger Löwenadler (*Captain Miller*); Eivor Landström (*Eva*); Erik "Hampe" Faustman & Bengt Ekerot (*freedom fighters*); Gösta Cederlund (*Sergej, a baker*); Ernst Brunman (*restaurant owner*); Torsten Hillberg (*colonel*); Frithiof Bjärne (*captain*).

SYNOPSIS & COMMENTARY: Between *The Strongest* (Den starkaste), the ambitious and sincere directorial debut of Alf Sjöberg (1903–1980) and his next (and first sound) film, *Life at Stake*, lay ten years of creative stage work and seemingly complete inactivity in the realm of the "Tenth Muse." Actually this infertile period for Sjöberg in film was one of many rejected screenplays and unsuccessful attempts to introduce bolder subjects and bolder ways of filming them. Sjöberg refused to compromise and to direct stereotyped, uninteresting pictures like the notorious *A Boarding House Named Paradise* (Pensionat Paradiset), 1937.

Life at Stake is set in an unnamed Baltic country, where revolutionaries are fighting against the army and the police. A young woman, Wanda, falls in love with a revolutionary, John. Max, who lives with Wanda, makes a living by illegal marketing of weapons, and Wanda helps him. Wanda delivers weapons (hidden in a baby carriage) to John without Max's knowledge. The revolutionaries cannot afford to pay for them. Wanda escapes from the headquarters of the revolutionaries, not wanting to expose them. She is actually playing a double game, because the authorities are informed about her activities. Wanda visits Sergej, a baker, with whom she shares interests and class-background, and there John finds her. Wanda reveals to him her double dealings. He wishes to abandon his political duties in order to show her his affection. In the meantime Max has discovered her falseness. He takes Chief of Police Miller to the headquarters of the revolutionaries. John's comrades are arrested. When John learns about their fate, he decides to complete his political mission. He abandons Wanda, who is arrested as well. John succeeds in performing his mission. The revolutionary forces brought in by him take the town. Max becomes desperate and shoots Wanda. John finds her. She dies in his arms.

The critics hailed the film as a complete and stunning novelty in the drab world of Swedish films of the time. Both the serious subject and the bold formal execution, hinting at a knowledge of the Russian classics and, above all, German expressionism, aroused interest in the young director's talent and hopes for his future work. However, the critics stressed the lack of precision in the development of individual threads and the ambiguity and vagueness of the situations. Most consistently outlined was the conflict raised by the double loyalties of John and Wanda, their love born in a world of meanness and moral filth. The film fascinated the more refined audiences. It proved how great Sjöberg's power of expression was at that time. He later became famous for his sophisticated taste in composition and his stormy visual temperament.

It seems that *Life at Stake* was received as a kind of allegory, topical when the picture was first released. The original story, by Swedish-Finnish writer Runar Schildt—written in 1919 and already filmed in 1938 by Nyrki Tapiovaara under the title *Stolen Death* (Varastettu kuolema)—was inspired by the Russian revolutionary movement in the early days of the century. But Sjöberg's film had more universal implications as a manifestation of the anxiety mounting in the Baltic countries in the 1939–1940 period, and as a reflection of the state of mind on the eve of the war that soon was to shake the world.

ABOVE: Revolutionaries conspire against the government. BELOW: Wanda gets acquainted with John.

ABOVE: John is not altogether friendly toward Max, Wanda's lover. BELOW: Max continues to impose himself on Wanda.

ABOVE: Max sends the government troops to round up the conspirators. BELOW: The whole group is arrested.

THE ROAD TO HEAVEN

(Swedish title: "Himlaspelet" [literally, "The Heavenly Play," which has also been used as an English-language release title].)

Produced 1942 by AB Wive Film. Released December 21, 1942.

Director: Alf Sjöberg. Screenplay (based on the play by Rune Lindström): Rune Lindström, Alf Sjöberg. Camera: Gösta Roosling. Art Director: Arne Åkermark. Music: Lille Bror Söderlundh. Editor: Oscar Rosander.

CAST: Rune Lindström (*Mats Ersson*); Eivor Landström (*Marit Knutsdotter*); Anders Henrikson (*Our Lord*); Holger Löwenadler (*King Solomon*); Gudrun Brost (*his mistress*); Emil Fjellström (*Old Jerk*); Arnold Sjöstrand (*Juvas Anders, a church painter*); Gunnar Sjöberg (*angel*); Björn Berglund (*Joseph*); Inga-Lilly Forsström (*Virgin Mary*); Hugo Björne (*Elijah*); Torsten Winge (*Jonah*); Frithiof Hedvall (*Isaiah*); Åke Claesson (*Jeremiah*); Lisskulla Jobs (*peasant woman*); Erik Hell (*Jon Persson*); Berta Hall (*his wife*); Tekla Sjöblom (*Mats's mother*); Carl Deurell (*lawman*); Gösta Folke (*curate*); Josua Bengtsson (*juryman*); Ernst Brunman (*innkeeper*); Anders Nyström (*shepherd boy*); Nils Gustafsson (*blind man by the roadside*); Harry Ahlin (*Garp Jesper*); Anita Björk (*Anna, his daughter*); John Ericsson, Torsten Lilliecrona & Henrik Schildt (*three peasants*); Börje Mellvig (*bellringer*); Helga Brofeldt (*old woman*); Tor Wallén & Harald Wehlnor (*two men*).

SYNOPSIS & COMMENTARY: Rune Lindström's naturalistic and purposely naïve play, successfully performed in the early Forties by the semiamateur Leksand troupe in the province of Dalecarlia and in guest performances at the Stockholm Royal Dramatic Theater, appealed to that theater's chief director, Alf Sjöberg.

After Marit Knutsdotter has been convicted as a witch and burnt at the stake, her fiancé Mats Ersson sets out "to Heaven" in search of justice. He is unaware that God, Who appears in the form of an elderly gentleman in frock coat and top hat, as Dalecarlian peasants imagine Him, had sent a peaceful death to her and taken her soul to Heaven. On his way, Mats meets the prophets Elijah, Isaiah and Jeremiah, and the newborn child Jesus with Mary and Joseph, and finally arrives at King Solomon's court. That is when Satan enters, submitting Mats to many trials and temptations. Mats gains wealth but in the process becomes a greedy, lecherous and brutal old man (in a magnificent and innovative sequence, Sjöberg shows the course of his aging). When the coachman of Death arrives, Mats tries to avoid Hell and recalls the faces and figures of the people in his life. God is merciful and takes him to Paradise. An idyllic shot of young Mats and Marit, reunited, ends the film.

It was feared that the intrusion of the film medium into the conventional texture of a traditional play would create dissonance. But Sjöberg's cooperation with Lindström, a versatile artist (writer, painter and actor) who was cast as Mats as he had been in the stage version, and with cameraman Gösta Roosling, a maker of romantic religious and folkloristic shorts, yielded a work worthy of the great tradition of Swedish film. The similarity to the golden age of silents is evident not only in the director's handling of individual scenes (the frenzied sleigh ride across icebound Siljan Lake was clearly patterned after the episode in Stiller's *Gösta Berling*) but above all in the similar approach to the scenery, to the sensualism of Nature, which constitutes an active background. The same threads of Scandinavian literature and religious tradition are emphasized here as those in the adaptations of *Jerusalem* and *The Phantom Carriage*. *The Road to Heaven*, originating from folk beliefs that the area of Siljan Lake was the center of the world and existence, and Paradise the homeland meadows (beliefs reflected in the famous Dalecarlia folk paintings), is a meditation on human life, an allegoric reflection on Everyman's fate. It also raises the perennial and ultimate questions about existence and destiny, virtue and crime, redemption and forgiveness, faith and doubt.

A similar religious problem in a different form, but also relating to the classic Swedish models, was to be handled in Molander's interesting adaptation of Kaj Munk's play *The Word* (Ordet) in 1943.

ABOVE: Merciful God brings Marit's soul to Heaven. BELOW: Shaken by the death of his fiancée, Mats sits at the local painter's place.

ABOVE: Mats on his way to "Heaven," searching for justice. BELOW: On his way Mats meets the prophets Elijah, Isaiah and Jeremiah.

ABOVE: He partakes in revelry at King Solomon's court. BELOW: In spite of Mats's sinful life, God allows him to enter Heaven.

TORMENT

(Swedish title: "Hets" [literally, "Persecution"]. British release title: "Frenzy.")

Produced 1944 by AB Svensk Filmindustri. Released October 2, 1944.

Director: Alf Sjöberg. Screenplay: Ingmar Bergman. Camera: Martin Bodin. Art Director: Arne Åkermark. Music: Hilding Rosenberg. Editor: Oscar Rosander.

CAST: Stig Järrel (*"Caligula," senior master of Latin*); Alf Kjellin (*Jan-Erik Widgren*); Mai Zetterling (*Bertha Olsson*); Olof Winnerstrand (*headmaster*); Gösta Cederlund (*"Pippi," a teacher*); Stig Olin (*Sandman*); Jan Molander (*Pettersson*); Olav Riégo (*Torsten Widgren, Jan-Erik's father*); Märta Arbin (*Mrs. Widgren*); Anders Nyström (*Bror Widgren*); Hugo Björne (*Dr. Nilsson*); Nils Dahlgren (*police inspector*); Gunnar Björnstrand, Nils Hultgren, Rune Landsberg & Richard Lund (*teachers*); Bertil Sohlberg (*"Knatten"*); Albert Ståhl (*"Sång-Pelle"*); Torsten Hillberg (*doctor at morgue*); John Zacharias (*his assistant*); Lillie Wästfeldt (*police matron*); Birger Malmsten (*Kreutz*); Greta Stave (*Selma, a housemaid*); Bengt Dalunde (*a young man*);Carl-Olof Alm, Rolf Bergström, Bengt van der Burg, Bengt Carenburg, Lars-Gunnar Carlsson, Curt Edgard, Claes Falkenberg, Sten Gester, Olle Gillström, Paul Granditsky, Carl-Einar Gregmar, Gunnar Hedberg-Carlsson, Lars Lindberg, Allan Linder, Lennart Nyberg, Bengt Persson, Arne Ragneborn, Sven Birger Strömsten, Gustaf Svensson & Tom Österholm (*senior high school students*).

AWARDS: Cannes (I, 1946): grand international prize. Film trophy "Charlie" of the newspaper *Aftontidningen* for the best Swedish film 1944/1945. First place in the magazine *Biografbladet* and the Association of Swedish Film Journalists' yearly voting 1944/1945.

SYNOPSIS & COMMENTARY: Sjöberg's next directing job after *The Road to Heaven* was to film a screenplay by Ingmar Bergman, a twenty-five-year-old assistant director of theater and opera who was a newly contracted script writer with SF. The subject was a conflict at a secondary school, partly reflecting the author's own experiences in the not-too-distant past. Like Sjöberg, but over a dozen years later, he had graduated from one of the Stockholm high schools.

The hero is the pupil Jan-Erik Widgren, who is close to graduation. The terror of the whole graduating class is a sadistic teacher of Latin nicknamed "Caligula." His conflict with Widgren is not limited to the school grounds. Going home one evening,

Jan-Erik comes across Bertha, a young salesclerk at the nearby tobacconist's, in a state of intoxication. He sees her home, and understanding and love begin to develop between the two. Bertha tells him of a mysterious persecutor whose frequent visits, during which she is forced to drink, scare her so much that she cannot sleep. Jan-Erik belittles her fears, thinking they are sickly delusions. When it is learned that "Caligula" is the mysterious man, it is too late; Bertha dies of a heart attack. "Caligula" is set free by the police for lack of evidence. His violent argument with Widgren causes Jan-Erik's expulsion from school only a few days before the final exams. Jan-Erik gets no support from his very strict parents, and goes to live in Bertha's room. Here, the old headmaster comes to visit with him. After their talk, Jan-Erik is able to face the future with more optimism.

In the early postwar years *Torment* was one of the best-known Swedish pictures, admired all over the world and given an award at the first (1946) Cannes festival.

The authenticity and youthful passion of the rebellion against school authorities is to the scriptwriter's credit. But the whole burden of working with the actors was Sjöberg's responsibility, and the final plastic shape of the work is evidently marked by his visual style. Swedish critic Lasse Bergström says in his essay on Sjöberg that the director was able to smooth out the over-convulsive style of the screenplay, thus giving the plot a psychologically credible background. Twelve years later Bergman was to write another script for Sjöberg about youngsters, *The Last Couple Out* (Sista paret ut), 1956.

In *Torment* the fundamental features of style are chiaroscuros, deformation of perspective, refined three-dimensional composition. The creative use of means already approved by German Expressionism is well motivated here. Apart from being a drama about a conflict of young people with their teacher (its release launched a series of still-topical discussions of teaching methods), *Torment* is above all a clear allegory of a tyrant whose ideological pedigree was even more obvious in 1944, prior to the final destruction of Nazism, than it is today. "Caligula's" methods are clearly of totalitarian origin and his pathological, fear-generating violence reflects the transformation that the German lower middle class underwent during the two decades between the world wars. In its review of the picture, the British *Monthly Film Bulletin* pointed out "Caligula's" physical resemblance to Himmler, who had also begun his career as a high-school teacher.

ABOVE: A school with a stern discipline [Gunnar Björnstrand as one of the teachers]. BELOW: The sadistic teacher nicknamed "Caligula" is the terror of the whole graduating class.

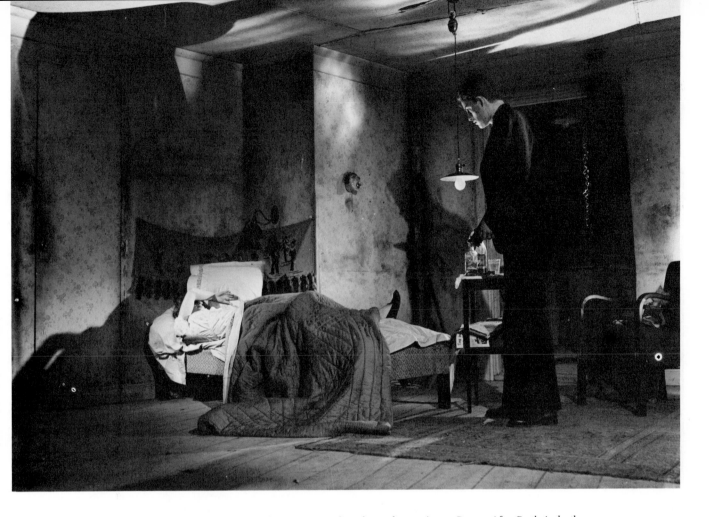

ABOVE: Jan-Erik Widgren visits the apartment of Bertha, a shop assistant. BELOW: After Bertha's death, Jan-Erik finds ''Caligula'' in her apartment.

ABOVE: Jan-Erik attacks "Caligula" in the headmaster's office, blaming him for the death of the girl. BELOW: Jan-Erik gets no support from his very strict parents.

THE DEVIL'S WANTON

(Swedish title: "Fängelse" [literally, "Imprisonment"].)

Produced 1949 by Lorens Marmstedt/Terrafilm. Released March 19, 1949.

Director: Ingmar Bergman. Screenplay: Ingmar Bergman. Camera: Göran Strindberg. Art Director: P. A. Lundgren. Music: Erland von Koch. Editor: Lennart Wallén.

CAST: Doris Svedlund (*Birgitta-Carolina Söderberg*); Birger Malmsten (*Tomas, a writer*); Eva Henning (*Sofi, his wife*); Hasse Ekman (*Martin Grandé, a film director*); Stig Olin (*Peter*); Irma Christensson (*Linnéa, Birgitta-Carolina's sister*); Anders Henrikson (*Paul, a former teacher of mathematics*); Marianne Löfgren (*Signe Bohlin, a boardinghouse landlady*); Curt Masreliez (*Alf*); Birgit "Bibi" Lindqvist (*Anna Bohlin, Signe's daughter*); Arne Ragneborn (*Anna's fiancé, a postman*); Carl-Henrik Fant (*Arne, an actor*); Inger Juel (*Greta, an actress*); Torsten Lilliecrona (*cameraman*); Segol Mann (*lighting technician*); Börje Mellvig (*inspector of police*); Åke Engfeldt (*police officer*); Åke Fridell (*Magnus, a guest at the boardinghouse*); Lasse Sarri (*Lasse*); Britta Brunius (*his mother*); Gunilla Klosterborg (*a dark lady*); Ulf Palme (*a man in a dream*).

SYNOPSIS & COMMENTARY: Ingmar Bergman, after his script-writing debut with *Torment*, continued with a variety of experiments: psychological drama in *Crisis* (Kris), 1945; an imitation of French poetic realism in *It Rains on Our Love* (Det regnar på vår kärlek), 1946; an allegory of unfulfilled daydreams in *A Ship to India/Frustration* (Skepp till Indialand), 1947; and an authentic description of a given environment, patterned after neorealist films, in *Port of Call* (Hamnstad), 1948. *The Devil's Wanton*, Bergman's sixth film, but the first made to his own, original scenario, blends all these threads and borrowed ideas into a consistent whole. It also develops the motifs of Bergman's scripts filmed by Gustaf Molander, *Woman Without a Face* (Kvinna utan ansikte), 1947, and *Eva*, 1948.

The dramaturgical frame of the picture is a meeting of motion-picture director Martin Grandé with his former teacher, Paul. Paul presents his idea for a screenplay in which evil, personified by Satan, is omnipotently governing the world. Martin laughs at the idea but passes it along to an alcoholic writer who, in turn, suggests another true-to-life idea. In a flashback embracing almost the whole film, we witness the life of Tomas who, having quarreled with his wife Sofi, lives in an old attic with the former prostitute Birgitta-Carolina. They find simple human bonds and happiness together. But Peter, Birgitta-Carolina's former "patron," and her sister Linnéa, who had forced her to drown her newborn baby, show up and blackmail her into returning to her former way of life. Seeing no way out, Birgitta-Carolina commits suicide by cutting her veins. At the end of the frame story, Martin and Paul agree that filming Birgitta-Carolina's story is impossible because it raises too many questions that have no answers.

In the pessimism of his moral play, Bergman was complying with certain typical trends of Swedish literature of the Forties which described "a world without mercy" and expressed fear, irresolution and uncertainty generated both by global events and by individual, psychological experience. The language of *The Devil's Wanton* possesses strong symbolical accents and is grim in its expression, reminding one rather of a nightmare than of reality. But some scenes are more optimistic, the ones that present the poetry of young love as the French saw it in their films. All the foreign influences and borrowings, as well as the famous farce screened in the attic with a primitive projector (not old footage but a scene Bergman staged to the pattern of old phantasmagorias by Méliès), prove that the director was already a keen observer of the history of motion pictures and already knew how to incorporate their accomplishments into his own, original vision.

The Devil's Wanton was Bergman's earliest film to be acknowledged by the world, beginning with the French critics (although this did not occur until years after its release, when his later masterpieces had paved the way). We find in it almost all the essential questions about man's existence that were later posed in a more complex way in *The Seventh Seal* and *Wild Strawberries*.

In 1949 Bergman worded them as follows: What was the guilt of Birgitta-Carolina for which she was sentenced to such a miserable life? And what was my own guilt and that of my neighbors? Are interference and prevention possible? Why the disabling helplessness in the face of evil?

ABOVE: Movie director Martin Grandé discusses a script idea with his former teacher, Paul. BELOW: Tomas quarrels with his wife Sofi.

ABOVE: He thinks that he has killed her. BELOW: He starts to live in an attic with an ex-prostitute, Birgitta-Carolina.

ABOVE: Birgitta-Carolina's former ''patron'' persuades her to take up prostitution again. BELOW: Birgitta-Carolina kills herself.

ONLY A MOTHER

(Swedish title: "Bara en mor.")

Produced 1949 by AB Svensk Filmindustri. Released October 31, 1949.

Director: Alf Sjöberg. Screenplay (based on the novel by Ivar Lo-Johansson): Alf Sjöberg, Ivar Lo-Johannsson. Camera: Martin Bodin. Art Director: Nils Svenwall. Music: Dag Wirén. Editor: Oscar Rosander.

CAST: Eva Dahlbeck (*Rya-Rya [Maria]*); Ragnar Falck (*Henrik, her husband*); Ulf Palme (*Hammar*); Åke Fridell (*farm inspector*); Hugo Björne (*Eniel*); Mona Geijer-Falkner (*Emili*); Max von Sydow (*Nils*); Margaretha Krook (*Berta*); Mimi Pollak (*Erika Rost*); Elsa Widborg (*cowherd's wife*); Olof Widgren (*Rya-Rya's father*); Signe Eklöf (*Rya-Rya's mother*); Ulla Smidje (*Cecilia*); Sif Ruud (*teacher*); Ernst Brunman (*chairman of the school council*); Gun Arvidsson (*Mathilda*); Birger Lensander (*Häger*); Erna Ovesen (*his wife*); Nils Hultgren (*Alm*); Ulf Andersson (*Otto as a child*); Jan-Olof Strandberg (*Otto 8 years later*); Björn Montin (*Elis as a child*); Sten Mattsson (*Elis 8 years later*); Hans Edelskog (*Stig*); Mona (Malm) Eriksson (*Anna*); Rita Sandström (*Anna as an adult*); Theodor Berthels (*peddler*); Svea Holm (*Adèle*); Birgit Hemmingson (*Jenny*); Arne Källerud (*photographer*); Gösta Qvist (*Håkansson*).

AWARD: Venice (XI, 1950): prize for best photography.

SYNOPSIS & COMMENTARY: Of the many screen versions of works by writers of the so-called Farmhand School, Sjöberg's *Only a Mother* was the most mature. Based on a novel by Lo-Johansson (born 1901), this multi-plot image of the life of a whole generation of hired farmhands concentrates on Rya-Rya. Almost from its beginning, her life is tinged with a nonconformism that is at variance with social norms. Her fiancé Nils, afraid of the villagers' scorn, parts with her when told she has bathed nude in the river. In her hurt confusion, Rya-Rya passively lets Henrik make love to her without loving him; she has a child by him and they get married. She is true to him all her life, except for one passionate night spent with the itinerant lumberjack Hammar. Ever after, Rya-Rya dedicates herself to her children and to exhausting and destructive hard labor. Years pass. Before dying at the hospital, Rya-Rya is able to enjoy the first successes of her growing children and to be spiritually reconciled with Henrik.

In 1949 the social problem of the agricultural proletariat did not exist any more. Therefore Sjöberg's film was received as a commemoration of that group, which numbered nearly half a million at the beginning of the nineteenth century. But even more, it is a personal drama of a woman whose desperate efforts to break out of the fettering limitations imposed by her environment are doomed to failure. However, the very fact that she makes the attempt gives the story a new, even more dramatic dimension. Thus the film is not so much a broad picture of prevailing customs —nor, as Danish critic Theodor Christensen interpreted it, a parallel to *The Road to Heaven* minus that film's religious trappings— as a psychologically pointed presentation of an individual's life. It is not the life of M. A. Nexö's Ditta, a helpless and passive victim of cruel circumstances, but the image of a woman of strong character, reluctant to yield to social prejudice and safeguarding her personality. It is no coincidence, Lasse Bergström comments, that Sjöberg's peculiar taste prompted him to depict the fate of people living in complete isolation both because of historic circumstances and because of their own individual psychical predilections. Nor is it a coincidence that this kind of isolation affects women more strongly than men. In some of his earlier films, and even more in his later ones, the director placed tragic female characters in the foreground: the titular heroines of *Iris* (Iris och löjtnantshjärta), 1947, *Miss Julie* and *Karin Månsdotter*, 1954.

ABOVE: Young and optimistic Rya-Rya expects to marry Nils. BELOW: Disappointed, she unwillingly gives herself to Henrik.

ABOVE: Her first baby is a fruit of this intimacy. BELOW: She secretly meets Hammar, with whom she spends the only adulterous night of her life.

ABOVE: The inspector tries to force her to make love to him. BELOW: Rya-Rya on her deathbed, surrounded by her family.

THE SUICIDE

(Swedish title: "Flicka och hyacinter" [literally, "Girl and Hyacinths"].)

Produced 1950 by Terra. Released March 6, 1950.

Director: Hasse Ekman. Screenplay: Hasse Ekman. Camera: Göran Strindberg. Art Director: Bibi Lindström. Music: Erland von Koch. Editor: Lennart Wallén.

CAST: Eva Henning (*Dagmar Brink, a bar pianist*); Ulf Palme (*Anders Wikner, a writer*); Birgit Tengroth (*Britt Wikner, his wife, advertising director of a publishing house*); Anders Ek (*Elias Körner, a painter*); Marianne Löfgren (*Gullan Wiklund, a music-hall artist*); Gösta Cederlund (*von Lieven, a banker*); Karl-Arne Holmsten (*Willy Borge, a popular singer*); Keve Hjelm (*Captain Stefan Brink, Dagmar's ex-husband*); Anne-Marie Brunius (*"Alex," the redheaded girl*); Björn Berglund (*Lövgren, a police inspector*); Gösta Gustafson (*the man with the etchings*); Georg Skarstedt (*a drunk*); Sven-Eric Gamble (*Kalle, a boy on the stairs*); Sigbrit Molin (*a girl on the stairs, his girl friend*); Gudrun Brost (*Körner's girl friend*); Sten Sture Modéen (*Hugge, proprietor of "Klara källare"*); Alf Östlund (*Viktor Ekberg, Gullan's husband*); Gustaf Hiort af Ornäs (*police doctor*); Åke Falck (*visitor at Körner's studio*); Astrid Bodin & Margit Andelius (*waitresses*); Svea Holst (*chambermaid at Dagmar Brink's place*); Gabriel Rosén (*a man at the bar*); Norma Sjöholm (*cigarette girl*); Marit Bergson (*visitor at Willy Borge's place*); Frithiof Bjärne (*police inspector*); Pia Strindberg (*a child on a tricycle*); Arne Lindblad (*a guest at "Klara källare"*); Tord Stål (*clergyman*); Gösta Bernhard (*night wanderer*).

AWARD: First place in the magazine *Biografbladet* and the Association of Swedish Film Journalists' yearly voting 1949/1950.

SYNOPSIS & COMMENTARY: Since his directorial debut in 1940, the young actor and director Hasse Ekman (born 1915), son of the famous actor Gösta Ekman, has produced sharp, satirical films as well as mediocre comedies and farces, serious war dramas and lyrical films about love. The last-named subject area, often under the influence of French poetic realism, seems to be most important for a proper evaluation of Ekman's talent and his importance for Swedish film art of the Forties and Fifties. While struggling to perfect his style, Ekman made, among other films, *Change of Trains* (Ombyte av tåg), 1943, *Wandering with the Moon* (Vandring med månen), 1945, and his most important work, shot in the same elegant, enigmatic narrative style full of delicate allusions: *The Suicide*.

A young woman, Dagmar Brink, commits suicide and wills all her property to her neighbor, a writer named Wikner. Intrigued by the situation and also looking for a topic for his next novel, Wikner—like the reporter in *Citizen Kane*—decides to solve Dagmar's enigma. In order to do that, he contacts a whole gallery of her old acquaintances, relatives and friends. These include her alleged father, bank manager von Lieven; the actress Gullan Wiklund, Dagmar's former roommate; her first husband, Stefan; the painter Körner; and the singer Willy Borge. All of them, in a series of flashbacks, show the writer (and the audience) a distinctive picture of Dagmar, a somewhat mysterious girl, difficult to comprehend, full of wishes and dreams that only she herself could be sure about. Borge maintains that Dagmar killed herself because of an unhappy love for him. Wikner, however, succeeds in proving that the object of her passionate and devastating feeling, leading to suicide, was none of the many men in the film, but a woman, the redheaded girl nicknamed "Alex."

Two tendencies fought each other in Ekman's films, one lyrical and optimistic, the other gloomy, seeking the dark secrets within the human mind and its subconscious and pitilessly mocking human weaknesses. Ekman was sometimes under the influence of his contemporary, Ingmar Bergman, but some of his better films were made before the most interesting works of his outstanding fellow director. A two-way influence is not altogether out of the question.

As in *Wandering with the Moon*, the main role in *The Suicide* was played by Ekman's wife at the time (his second), Eva Henning, who some years later was to leave Sweden for Norway and marry the well-known actor Toralv Maurstad. The role of Dagmar was not only written especially for her, but was to be the most complete revelation of the real personality of this actress, whom even in real life nobody could fully know. Such an attempt to portray Eva Henning was probably no indifferent task for the director. Thus he put into this, his most ambitious work, a lot of real creative verve, attaining unusually fine shades of psychological truth and extending the ramifications of the plot in both depth and breadth.

The Suicide, a film based on an authentic case but never becoming a debate on homosexuality, was expensive to make and lost the producers about 100,000 Swedish crowns, but it was highly praised by critics at home and has been recognized as one of the minor masterpieces of the Swedish cinema.

ABOVE: Dagmar Brink, whose suicide mystifies all the people that knew her. BELOW: Her alleged father, bank manager von Lieven.

ABOVE: Her former husband (at the right). BELOW: The painter Elias Körner.

ABOVE: The singer Willy Borge. BELOW: The real love of her life, and cause of her death, was an enigmatic girl nicknamed "Alex."

ONE SUMMER OF HAPPINESS

(Swedish title: "Hon dansade en sommar" [literally, "She Danced One Summer"].)

Produced 1951 by Nordisk Tonefilm. Released December 17, 1951.

Director: Arne Mattsson. Screenplay (based on the novel by Per-Olof Ekström): Volodja Semitjov. Camera: Göran Strindberg. Art Director: Bibi Lindström. Music: Sven Sköld. Editor: Lennart Wallén.

CAST: Ulla Jacobsson (*Kerstin, a farm girl*); Folke Sundquist (*Göran Stendal*);Edvin Adolphson (*Anders Persson, a farmer, Göran's uncle*); Irma Christensson (*Sigrid, his sister*); John Elfström (*clergyman*); Erik Hell (*Torsten, a farm hand*); Sten Lindgren (*Stendal, Göran's father*); Nils Hallberg (*Nisse, a young farm worker*); Gösta Gustafson (*Berndt Larsson, Kerstin's uncle*); Berta Hall (*Anna, his wife*); Sten Mattsson (*Olle, a young farm worker*); Arne Källerud (*Viberg*); Gunvor Pontén (*Sylvia, Nisse's girl friend*); Axel Högel (*grandfather*); Hedvig Lindby (*grandmother*); Erich Conard (*Helge, Göran's schoolmate*); Margareta Löwler (*Mary Ann, Göran's girl friend in town*); Olav Riégo (*teacher*); Ulla-Bella Fridh & Gunilla Pontén (*other schoolmates of Göran*); Carl-Gustaf Lindstedt (*concertina player*); John Melin & Gustaf "Stålfarfar" Håkansson (*patients at the hospital*).

AWARDS: Cannes (V, 1952): prize for best musical score. Berlin (II, 1952): Grand Prize (Golden Bear).

SYNOPSIS & COMMENTARY: Arne Mattsson (born 1919), the most prolific of still-active Swedish directors (fifty-three films), began his career as a scriptwriter and assistant to director Per Lindberg. One of the last pictures of the prematurely deceased Lindberg contained a short scene in which the new starlet Viveca Lindfors initiated the long series of Scandinavian sensual baths in the open. It was a kind of a surprise when Mattsson repeated that bath scene ten years later in an artistically perfect and complete way, stunning nearly the whole world and establishing the general idea about Scandinavian erotic freedom.

The principal character is Göran Stendal, who is spending his vacation after graduation from high school at his uncle's place in the countryside. He meets Kerstin, a girl brought up very strictly by her uncle and aunt on the neighboring farm. These old people's views on education are shared by the local pastor, the terror of local youth. Göran's uncle, Anders Persson, is different; he advocates young people's freedom and makes one of his buildings available to them for meetings and rehearsals of their amateur theater. Göran and Kerstin fall deeply in love, her foster parents and Göran's father strongly objecting to the relationship. The two young people spend the night together by a lake in the woods, bathing in the nude. Soon afterward, they take part in a successful performance at the local theater and are blissfully happy. When Göran takes the girl for a ride on his motor bike, they have an accident and she dies. Göran is unable to stand the pastor's accusing, hypocritical speech at the funeral. He runs back to *their* lake, where he can remember his beloved in privacy.

The film doubtless had a touch of sentimentality, but its violent attack on provincial—mainly clerical—hypocrisy introduced a new accent in the Swedish cinema. In the whole arrangement of the conflict and in the visual approach to some of the key scenes, Mattsson's picture is reminiscent of another work that defied traditional morality. Like Claude Autant-Lara's film from Raymond Radiguet's novel *Devil in the Flesh* (Le diable au corps), *One Summer of Happiness* made censors everywhere hesitate, though on the other hand it was a turning point that helped to overcome puritan constraints. The censors in Sweden, Denmark and Norway permitted the release of the picture without cuts; in England only minor cuts were made in the most drastic scenes; some other countries, among them Canada and Spain, banned the film. The Swedish producer prepared abbreviated versions for some countries.

From the narrowly artistic point of view, Mattsson's film does not even reach the level of Bergman's less important pictures (although Mattsson did recall the valuable traditions of Scandinavian film art in which Northern nature plays a significant role), such as *Illicit Interlude* (Sommarlek), 1950, but it became the Swedish cinema's biggest box-office hit. It was sold to over a hundred countries and is still being reissued—uncut, of course. It won prizes at international festivals. The fact that the majority of motion-picture fans abroad associated it with their concept of Sweden as the homeland of erotic libertinism, and that the picture also operated as an advertisement for touring in Sweden, should not discredit its basically honest authors.

ABOVE: Göran Stendal meets Kerstin during his summer vacation. BELOW: They work together in the fields.

ABOVE: The local clergyman does not approve of the young people's spare-time activities. BELOW: Göran and Kerstin spend the night together, bathing nude.

ABOVE: Kerstin is killed in a motor-bike accident. BELOW: Göran observes her funeral at a distance.

MISS JULIE

(Swedish title: "Fröken Julie.")

Produced 1951 by Sandrew. Released July 30, 1951.

Director: Alf Sjöberg. Screenplay (based on the play by August Strindberg): Alf Sjöberg. Camera: Göran Strindberg. Art Director: Bibi Lindström. Music: Dag Wirén. Editor: Lennart Wallén.

CAST: Anita Björk (*Miss Julie*); Ulf Palme (*Jean, a servant*); Märta Dorff (*Kristin the cook, Jean's girl friend*); Anders Henrikson (*Count Carl, Julie's father*); Lissi Alandh (*Countess Berta, Julie's mother*); Inger Norberg (*Julie as a child*); Jan Hagerman (*Jean as a child*); Kurt-Olof Sundström (*Julie's fiancé*); Inga Gill (*Viola*); Åke Fridell (*Robert, a brick manufacturer*); Max von Sydow (*stableman*); Margaretha Krook (*governess*); Åke Claesson (*doctor*); Sture Ericson (*Jean's father*); Svea Holst (*Jean's mother*); Signe Lundberg-Settergren, Helga Brofeldt, Ingrid Björk & Maud Walter (*servant girls*); Olle Ståhl (*servant*); Gösta Qvist (*hunter*); John Hilke (*clergyman*); Åke Björling (*soldier*); Bengt Sundmark, Gregor Dahlman & Olof Ekblad (*farmhands*); Torgny Anderberg (*manager*); Eric Laurent (*policeman*); Martin Ljung (*forester, Julie's dancing partner*); Erik Forslund (*coachman*); Marianne Karlbeck (*nursemaid*); Karl Andersson (*servant*); Agda Helin (*midwife*).

AWARDS: Cannes (IV, 1951): Grand Prix (Golden Palm), shared with *Miracolo a Milano*. First place in the magazine *Biografbladet* and the Association of Swedish Film Journalists' yearly poll 1951/1952. Punta del Este (1952): Uruguayan film critics' honorary mention for best photography and direction; Buenos Aires Cinema Club nomination for the best film. New York Film Critics' honorary award 1954. First place in the magazine *Chaplin*'s poll 1964 for the best Swedish sound film of all time.

SYNOPSIS & COMMENTARY: Ever since Strindberg's famous permission, "You may film as many of my works as you wish," given only a few months before his death, very few of his plays and stories were filmed in his native country (in France *The Dance of Death* was produced with Erich von Stroheim starring). In adapting *Miss Julie* in 1950, Alf Sjöberg decided —according to Swedish film historian Rune Waldekranz—to modernize the interpretation of the play, which belongs to Strindberg's naturalistic period preceding his later visionary works such as *A Dream Play*.

It is Midsummer Eve. On the count's estate the servants and farmhands are dancing in the barn to the sounds of violin, accordion and clarinet. The count himself is paying a visit to a neighbor, and his daughter, Miss Julie, is at home alone. Agitated by the music and the laughter, she goes to the barn, where she invites the count's groom Jean to dance with her. But soon she finds him dull, and leaves him embarrassed and a bit humiliated. He joins his fiancée, the cook Kristin, in the estate's kitchen. Miss Julie follows him there and begins a frivolous love scene with him. Jean tells her how even in his adolescence he used to dream about her, the young mistress of the estate, although he was only a poor farmhand's boy. His words become a passionate declaration of love and under the enchantment of Midsummer Night she gives herself to him. After the seduction Julie becomes aware of the enormity of her behavior. She tells Jean in turn about her unsettled childhood and the factors that made her a neurotic, unsatisfied woman. Jean boasts of his big plans: he is going to escape with Julie to Italy and Switzerland, to begin a new life, but Julie understands that this is just an unrealistic dream. When her father returns to the castle at dawn, the terrible truth is apparent to her. There is just one way out—suicide— and Miss Julie cuts her throat with a razor.

All of the action of the play *Miss Julie* takes place in the kitchen of the heroine's family manor; this permits the concentration and intensity typical of the theater of the three unities. Sjöberg, who had preserved these unities in his 1945 stage production of the work, decided to set the film in a variety of interiors and exteriors and to fragment the narrative into an intricate time arrangement. He also emulated the modern simultaneous theater as exemplified by such Strindberg plays as *The Ghost Sonata* in which the stage is populated simultaneously by living people, spirits and ghosts. Without giving up the dramatic possibilities of the confrontation between Jean, the servant climbing up the social ladder, and the whimsical, neurotic Miss Julie, who symbolizes the decadence and fall of the aristocracy, Sjöberg attempted to penetrate the two characters' past and its significance for their present problems. And to show the past and present on one level he did not hesitate to use a means revolutionary in the history of the cinema: showing "now" and "then" in one and the same shot. And so we see Julie telling of her childhood and in the same frame Julie as a child, sensitive and nervous, her behavior explaining many of the adult Julie's traits. Analogous scenes with Jean, the farmhand driven from the estate, point to his inferiority complex, his rankling lust for revenge and his persistence in rising from the lowest stratum of society. Miss Julie's suicide at the end is meant to symbolize the departure of a former social class. Sjöberg was almost as much interested in the passing of an epoch of civilization as in Strindberg's naturalistic treatment of the struggle between species (here, the sexes) where the stronger survives, and in the problem of women's emancipation used in the film to balance the social chasm between Julie and Jean.

Miss Julie was unanimously ranked as one of the best Scandinavian pictures of all time. It is to date the only Swedish picture to win the Gold Palm in Cannes. Sjöberg was never able again to repeat its all-round success. In his later films he occasionally tends to quote from himself, placing characters from different time periods in one and the same shot—as in *The Island* (Ön), 1966, and in a painstakingly produced but insipid adaptation of *The Father* (1969). But these pictures lack the author's old visual power that combined Sjöström's folk traditions with Stiller's masterly visual skill, vigor and impetus.

ABOVE: Establishing shot: a symbol of Miss Julie's confinement in her world. BELOW: Jean and Julie dancing in the barn.

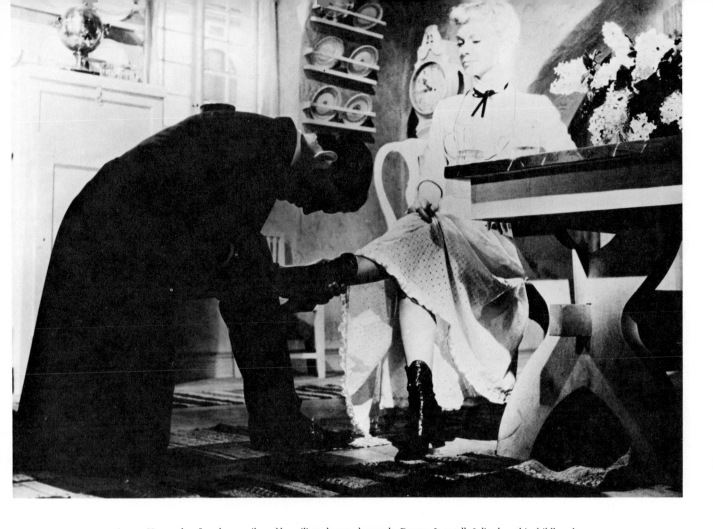

ABOVE: Upper-class female prevails and humiliates lower-class male. BELOW: Jean tells Julie about his childhood.

ABOVE: Julie tells Jean how she was raised by a domineering mother. BELOW: The count arrives too late, after Julie's suicide.

THE NAKED NIGHT

(Swedish title: "Gycklarnas afton" [literally, "The Evening of the Clowns"]. British release title: "Sawdust and Tinsel.")

Produced 1953 by Sandrew. Released September 14, 1953.

Director: Ingmar Bergman. Screenplay: Ingmar Bergman. Camera: Sven Nykvist, Hilding Bladh. Art Director: Bibi Lindström. Music: Karl-Birger Blomdahl. Editor: Caro-Olov Skeppstedt.

CAST: Åke Grönberg (*Albert Johansson, owner of the circus*); Harriet Andersson (*Anne, the equestrienne*); Hasse Ekman (*Frans, an actor*); Anders Ek (*Teodor Frost, a clown*); Gudrun Brost (*Alma, his wife*); Annika Tretow (*Agda, Albert's wife*); Gunnar Björnstrand (*Sjuberg, the theater manager*); Erik Strandmark (*Jens*); Kiki (*the midget*); Majken Torkell (*Mrs. Ekberg*); Vanje Hedberg (*her son*); Curt Löwgren (*Blom*); Åke Fridell (*officer*); Conrad Gyllenhammar (*Fager*); Mona Sylwan (*Mrs. Fager*); Hanny Schedin (*Aunt Asta*); Mikael Fant (*Anton*); Sigvard Thörnqvist (*Meijer*); Naemi Briese (*Mrs. Meijer*); Lissi Alandh, Karl-Axel Forsberg, Olav Riégo, John Starck, Erna Groth & Agda Helin (*actors & actresses*); Julie Bernby (*tightrope dancer*); John Björling (*Uncle Greven*); Gunborg Larsson (*Mrs. Tanti*); Göran Lundqvist & Mats Hådell (*boys*).

AWARDS: Etoile de Cristal de l'Académie du Cinéma (Paris) 1957, and prize for the performance of Åke Grönberg. Buenos Aires (1958): Certificate of Merit. West German film critics' grand prize 1958 for direction. Shared second prize for best foreign film in Polish Film Critics' Association's yearly poll 1959.

SYNOPSIS & COMMENTARY: In Ingmar Bergman's pictures, the problem of an artist's status and the role he performs in a given social environment has a special place. For this analysis the author often reaches back into the more or less distant past, using conventional historical costumes, old literature and bygone forms of entertainment, such as the shows once put on by jugglers and acrobats to amuse the magnates. Whether the "performer" is Johansson the ringmaster, Vogler in *The Magician/The Face* (Ansiktet), 1958, or even Pastor Ericsson in *Winter Light* (Nattvardsgästerna), 1963, he is always helpless, often humiliated. Bergman has compassion for the jugglers tossed from place to place, chased and persecuted in the name of love for mankind. It is no coincidence that a troupe of tightrope dancers is spared from the plague in *The Seventh Seal*. Bergman ennobles the jugglers as human beings and as artists, showing the victories they win while paying a high price for them, and the failures they have to live with.

In the first scenes of *The Naked Night*, a circus van slowly moves forward on a cool, cloudy morning at the beginning of the twentieth century. Jens, the driver, is telling Johansson, the manager of the circus who is worried by insomnia and financial problems, about a tragicomical adventure that befell the aging wife of Frost, the clown. Some drunken officers made her bathe nude in the sea. In bright, overexposed photography, intensified by the impressive background music of Karl-Birger Blomdahl, we actually see the scene of cruelty, debasement and humiliation.

The circus arrives at a provincial town in Scania. Johansson plans to advertise with a triumphant street parade in which the circus personnel will appear in costumes that Johansson hopes to borrow from the local theater. Anne, the equestrienne, who has been his mistress for several years, accompanies him on the visit to the theater manager. Despite the scorn this manager has and displays for the "lower kind" that the circus people are in his opinion, he agrees to lend the costumes. At the theater Anne meets Frans, an actor and reckless seducer. A few hours later she sleeps with him. Albert Johansson in the meantime pays a visit to his wife Agda, who lives in that town, but his indecision about quitting circus life clashes with Agda's relentless attitude; she has no more illusions and is now fully able to continue on her own. At night, while the show is on and enjoying unusual success, Albert confronts Frans. The circus man, big and strong, has to yield physically to the actor, who uses his fists coldly, with calculated technique. Albert loses the fight and is humiliated in front of the whole circus troupe. His attempt at suicide also ends in failure. The next morning Anne, whom Frans has promised to rescue from her drab circus existence, joins Albert and they move on in the circus van together.

"In this picture," one of the Scandinavian reviewers commented, "Bergman seized something of the very essence of life; he leaves man with a feeling of a sense of existence even after he has been through all the plagues this world's purgatory has to offer."

ABOVE: On a circus van that slowly moves forward. BELOW: Jens, the driver, tells Johansson, the manager, about Mrs. Frost, who was provoked by drunken officers to take a nude bath in the sea.

ABOVE: The circus arrives at a provincial town in Scania. BELOW: Anne, the equestrienne, becomes acquainted with Frans, an actor and reckless seducer.

ABOVE: The cruel fight in the arena. BELOW: The naked night is coming to an end.

THE GREAT ADVENTURE

(Swedish title: "Det stora äventyret.")

Produced 1953 by Arne Sucksdorff-Sandrew. Released September 29, 1953.

Direction, Screenplay, Cinematography & Editing: Arne Sucksdorff. Music: Lars Erik Larsson.

CAST: Anders Norberg (*Anders*); Kjell Sucksdorff (*Kjell*); Arne Sucksdorff (*Father*). Narration: Gunnar Sjöberg.

AWARDS: Cannes (VII, 1954): international prize, honorary certificate for Sucksdorff and prize of the Commission Supérieure Technique du Cinéma. Berlin (IV, 1954): big silver plate for documentary film and mention of the Office Catholique International du Cinéma. Référendum International de Vichy (1960): special mention.

SYNOPSIS & COMMENTARY: Swedish documentary films are usually associated with Arne Sucksdorff (born 1917). After work as a (still) photographer, he got his first job with motion pictures in the late Thirties and soon became the leading director of Swedish shorts. His first films were the result of patient and methodical hunts with the camera, the result above all of his preference for outdoor life and his special knack for coexistence with nature. His pantheistic approach to nature and his reluctance to accept urban civilization later had a dominating impact on Sucksdorff's creative work.

In the many shorts produced during the period 1939–1951, Sucksdorff showed nature in the lushness of her genuine beauty, well aware at the same time that the laws of natural selection that govern it are cruel. Among these shorts were *The Gull* (Trut!), 1944, and *A Divided World* (En kluven värld), 1948. The subject of other Sucksdorff documentaries is man's interference in the world of nature: *Shadows on the Snow* (Skuggor över snön), 1945. In *Rhythm of a City* (Människor i stad), Academy Award winner, 1948, and *Moving On* (Uppbrott), 1948, he is just as keen a reporter of the life in various human environments.

His first full-length film, *The Great Adventure*, is an anthology of subjects typical of his earlier work. He spent over two years shooting 80,000 meters of film, eventually editing only 2,500 into the final version. In the slight fictional framework, Sucksdorff shows how the secrets of nature are perceived by the innocent eyes of two little boys, Anders and Kjell, a farmer's sons in central Sweden. The boys witness the passing seasons, the interactions of nature governed by its own rules, the coming and going of species. Wild animals fight for survival in the vicinity of the farm. One winter the boys catch an otter and keep it in a cage in one of the farm buildings, secretly taming and feeding it. When spring comes, the boys take the otter for walks and let it bathe in the lake. One day, taking advantage of an unguarded moment, the otter disappears. When the farm workers celebrate the coming of the summer, the boys mourn the loss of their pet. But when they see a flock of cranes heading north on their return from their winter migration, they realize that "the great adventure" is only beginning.

Sucksdorff's camera recorded the whole cycle of nature's changes as he keenly observed the wealth of activity in the woods.

The Great Adventure was quite successful with both audiences and critics. The tradition of spending leisure time outdoors in strenuous and skillful sports is very strong in Sweden, and this is one of the reasons documentaries on animal life are well liked. *The Great Adventure* is one of the features reissued quite frequently in theaters, and even more often on TV. It won prizes at the Cannes and Berlin festivals and was distributed in many countries.

After a few years Sucksdorff began to work in faraway countries. He produced a few shorts and a color feature—*The Flute and the Arrow* (En djungelsaga), 1957—in India; in 1965, *My Home Is Copacabana* (Mitt hem är Copacabana); and films for TV in the Mato Grosso. Denied the possibility of working with Swedish producers, Sucksdorff left his country many years ago. Marrying a South American Indian woman, he moved to the tropics, just as another artist, Gauguin, had once moved to the South Seas. Sucksdorff apparently wanted to prove that the contrasts of nature can also be a motive power for creativity. But he always remained true to his simple, childlike approach to the world of nature, uncontaminated by civilization. This proves that Sucksdorff is related to such poets of the documentary camera as Robert Flaherty and Georges Rouquier.

ABOVE: Spring has come to the forest. BELOW: The fox cubs are eager for their dinner.

ABOVE: The vixen on her hunting tour. BELOW: Playful otters and the fish they have caught.

ABOVE: Anders with his pet. BELOW: The only surviving fox of the litter attempts to cope with the hard winter conditions.

SMILES OF A SUMMER NIGHT

(Swedish title: "Sommarnattens leende.")

Produced 1955 by AB Svensk Filmindustri. Released December 26, 1955.

Director: Ingmar Bergman. Screenplay: Ingmar Bergman. Camera: Gunnar Fischer. Art Director: P. A. Lundgren. Music: Erik Nordgren. Editor: Oscar Rosander.

CAST: Gunnar Björnstrand (*Fredrik Egerman*); Ulla Jacobsson (*Anne, his wife*); Eva Dahlbeck (*Desirée Armfeldt, an actress*); Björn Bjelvenstam (*Henrik Egerman, Fredrik's son*); Naima Wifstrand (*Lady Armfeldt, Desirée's mother*); Anders Wulff (*Fredrik, Desirée's son*); Jarl Kulle (*Count Carl Magnus Malcolm*); Margit Carlquist (*Charlotte, his wife*); Harriet Andersson (*Petra, the maid*); Åke Fridell (*Frid, the coachman*); Birgitta Valberg & Bibi Andersson (*actresses*); Gösta Prüzelius, Sten Gester & Mille Schmidt (*servants*); Jullan Kindahl (*Beata, Egerman's cook*); Gull Natorp (*Malla, Desirée's maid*); Gunnar Nielsen (*Niklas, Malcolm's orderly*); Yngve Nordwall (*Ferdinand*); Hans Strååt (*Adolf Almgren, a photographer*); Lisa Lundholm (*Mrs. Almgren*); Börje Mellvig, George Adelly & Carl-Gustaf Lindstedt (*solicitors*); Ulf Johansson, Georg Skarstedt, Ingmar Bergman (*solicitor's assistants*); David Eriksson (*tobacconist*); Sigge Fürst (*police officer*); Arne Lindblad (*actor*).

AWARDS: Cannes (IX, 1956): prize for poetic humor. The newspaper *Svenska Dagbladet*: plate for best film, 1956. The magazine *FIB*: prizes 1955 for best film, direction, screenplay, feminine main role (Eva Dahlbeck) and supporting role (Harriet Andersson).

SYNOPSIS & COMMENTARY: In the early Fifties Ingmar Bergman produced his first comedies. To the successful re-creation of an environment in his early films (*Crisis* and *Port of Call*) he added irony, satire and sarcasm. A team of stage actors under Bergman's guidance began to take the lead in these films. The pair of experienced lovers appearing in them were Eva Dahlbeck and Gunnar Björnstrand. From the comedy-drama *Secrets of Women* (Kvinnors väntan; in England, *Waiting Women*), containing the classic and frequently cited elevator scene, to *A Lesson in Love* (En lektion i kärlek), to the stylized *Smiles of a Summer Night*, these two artists were subject to incessant clashes, the success of which was due mainly to the perfect adjustment of their acting temperaments and the director's perfect knowledge of the psychology of the game of love, particularly from the woman's angle. The author of *Persona* has revealed this knowledge in many of his pictures.

Smiles of a Summer Night takes place in Sweden during the *belle époque*. Although Fredrik Egerman, a lawyer, has been married to young Anne for two years, their marriage has still not been consummated. Fredrik has an adolescent son from his first marriage, Henrik, whose awakening sensuality makes him cast passionate and lusty glances at not only Petra, the maid, but also his good-looking stepmother. Egerman still cherishes the memory of the actress Desirée Armfeldt, who was once his mistress. During a chance visit of Fredrik to her house, her new lover Count Malcolm suddenly shows up. Desirée's mother invites the Egermans and the Malcolms to a party, and serves a special liquor with allegedly magic properties. Henrik Egerman, brought to despair by the libertinism of all the others present and his own sexual immaturity, attempts suicide. Chance brings him to the bedroom of his sleeping stepmother. They make love and confess their mutual fondness, and soon Frid the coachman and Petra help the two in a romantic escape by coach. This escape is observed by the stunned lawyer, who has just parted with Countess Malcolm. When (on a haystack) Frid tells Petra the secret of the three smiles of Midsummer Night, a tragicomic culmination takes place. The Count summons the lawyer to a Russian roulette duel. The gun Egerman holds to his temple goes off, but the load was just soot. The Malcolms are reconciled and Egerman stays with Desirée, whose little son's name is also Fredrik.

Bergman's multitude of clever little psychological observations, the bright dialogue and refinedly funny situations make the film outstanding in its category. Many experts tend to see Bergman as an artist who preserved and improved the traditions of Mauritz Stiller's style, especially that of his classic comedy *Erotikon*. But *Smiles*, awarded a special prize for its poetical humor at Cannes (1956), remained an isolated success in Bergman's career. None of his later comedies has reached as high a level: both *The Devil's Eye* (Djävulens öga) and *All These Women* (För att inte tala om alla dessa kvinnor) were a disappointment to the admirers of the Swedish master's talent. But in February 1973, eighteen years after *Smiles* had been produced, a musical opened on Broadway with a libretto directly derived from the script Bergman had written for this picture: *A Little Night Music*.

ABOVE: Egerman visits Desirée backstage. BELOW: Desirée's mother agrees to invite her daughter's friends to a party.

ABOVE: The Malcolms arrive at the Armfeldt estate. BELOW: The table conversation sparkles with wit just before Lady Armfeldt introduces her drink with allegedly magic properties.

ABOVE: The love game begins between Frid, the coachman, and Petra, the maid. BELOW: Malcolm and Egerman at the Russian roulette duel.

THE SEVENTH SEAL

(Swedish title: "Det sjunde inseglet.")

Produced 1955 by AB Svensk Filmindustri. Released February 16, 1957.

Director: Ingmar Bergman. Screenplay (based on his own play): Ingmar Bergman. Camera: Gunnar Fischer. Art Director: P. A. Lundgren. Music: Erik Nordgren. Editor: Lennart Wallén.

CAST: Max von Sydow (*Antonius Block, a knight*); Inga Landgré (*Karin, his wife*); Gunnar Björnstrand (*Jöns, his squire*); Nils Poppe (*Jof, a juggler*); Bibi Andersson (*Mia, his wife*); Tommy Karlsson (*their son*); Bengt Ekerot (*Death*); Åke Fridell (*Plog, a blacksmith*); Inga Gill (*Lisa, his wife*); Erik Strandmark (*Jonas Skat*); Bertil Anderberg (*Raval*); Gunnel Lindblom (*girl*); Anders Ek (*monk*); Maud Hansson (*witch*); Gunnar Olsson (*church painter*); Lars Lind (*young monk*); Benkt-Åke Benktsson (*innkeeper*); Tor Borong (*peasant at the inn*); Catherine Berg & Mona Malm (*two young women*); Ulf Johansson (*leader of the squires*); Sten Ardenstam & Gordon Löwenadler (*two squires*); Harry Asklund (*merchant*); Gudrun Brost (*woman at the inn*); Josef Norman & Nils Whiten (*old men*).

AWARDS: Cannes (X, 1957): special prize of the jury (Silver Palm) shared with Wajda's *Kanal*. The magazine *FIB:* silver prize for the film and for Gunnar Björnstrand's performance. First place in the Swedish critics' poll 1957. Best Swedish film in the poll of the magazine *Fickjournalen* 1957. Grand Prix du film d'avant-garde in the French poll of the Inventaire du Cinéma 1958. Second place on the *Saturday Review* list 1958. Fourth place on the *New York Post* list 1958. Tenth place on the Canadian Broadcasting Corporation list 1958. One of the ten best films on the *New York Times* list 1958. The Trofeo of the Federación Nacional de Cineclubs, Valladolid, 1960. The Nastro d'Argento (Italy) 1961 for best foreign film.

SYNOPSIS & COMMENTARY: After the international success of *Smiles of a Summer Night*, Bergman could afford to be discriminating in the choice of subjects for his films. He no longer had to compromise with producers, since he had become an asset even from the point of view of box office. His next film, *The Seventh Seal*, was a milestone that established the director's position as one of the most prominent film authors of modern times.

For this film Bergman was inspired by the impressions of his youth when, accompanying his father, a pastor, he visited village churches in the neighborhood of Stockholm and could admire their characteristic paintings (the Dalecarlia parallels of these paintings had earlier inspired Sjöström and Sjöberg to produce *Sons of Ingmar* and *The Road to Heaven*, respectively). Bergman first wrote a one-act play on the subject; directed by Bengt Ekerot, it was staged in Malmö and Stockholm in 1955. He later converted it into a screenplay.

The Seventh Seal is the first mature manifestation of Bergman's interest in the problem of faith and doubt, in such ultimate matters as the fear of death and of the Last Judgment, in a search for God and a justification of human existence. The protagonist of this morality play set in the Middle Ages is Antonius Block. After ten years of absence he returns to Sweden from a crusade to the Holy Land. In the course of the film he plays a game of chess with Death and meditates about faith in conversations with himself, with an alleged witch sentenced to be burned at the stake, and with the confessor at the village church. This confessor is none other than Death, who deceitfully traps the knight into revealing what his next move on the chessboard will be. Block's doubts are Manichean in nature: in the face of God's silence he is prepared to get the secret of existence even from Satan. When Block and his squire Jöns, a coarse clodhopper and a nonbeliever, get back to Sweden, a plague is ravaging the country. They see collective panic and despair, people mortifying themselves (a parade of flagellants) and raving fanaticism. A notable exception in this grim tableau is a family of itinerant jugglers, Jof, Mia and their child. They are the symbol of universal innocence and good, a counterpart to the Holy Family (Joseph and Mary). They will be the ones saved from the plague when —upon Block's return to his family castle and the reading of verses from the Apocalypse during the last supper ("and when the Lamb broke the seventh seal")—merciless Death draws the other characters into a last dance which Jof sees on the horizon. Was Bergman perhaps saying that all the world's evil, plague and death are only part of a tightrope dancer's vision? The end of the film also seems to paraphrase the *Phantom Carriage* theme contained in the final words: "Prepare thy soul for the day the Reaper cometh."

The international response to the film, which among other awards won the jury's special prize at Cannes in 1957 (*ex aequo* with Andrzej Wajda's *Kanal*), reconfirmed the author's high rank and proved that *The Seventh Seal*, regardless of its degree of accuracy in reproducing medieval scenery, may be considered as a universal, timeless allegory. It speaks to all of us of the tragic fate of people shackled by religion, and of the threat of mankind's total extermination in a nuclear war. From this film onward, world critics were to consider Bergman as an author presenting the grave problems of modern times in the form of broad pictures that not only investigated the psychological intricacies of individual lives but also told, obsessively, of the irrevocability of man's destiny and the loneliness of living within predetermined uncrossable limits.

ABOVE: Antonius Block plays a game of chess with Death. BELOW: Death, disguised as the confessor at the village church, traps Block into revealing his next move on the chessboard.

ABOVE: Block and Jöns observe mass panic and raging fanaticism in the face of the plague. BELOW: Jof and Mia, itinerant jugglers, giving a performance with Jonas Skat.

ABOVE: Many of the characters convene at Block's castle, where they wait in prayer. BELOW: Finally Death draws them all into a dance.

WILD STRAWBERRIES

(Swedish title: "Smultronstället" [literally, "The Wild Strawberry Patch"].)

Produced 1957 by AB Svensk Filmindustri. Released December 26, 1957.

Director: Ingmar Bergman. Screenplay: Ingmar Bergman. Camera: Gunnar Fischer. Art Director: Gittan Gustafsson. Music: Erik Nordgren. Editor: Oscar Rosander.

CAST: Victor Sjöström (*Professor Isak Borg*); Gunnar Björnstrand (*Evald, his son*); Ingrid Thulin (*Marianne, Evald's wife*); Bibi Andersson (*Sara*); Folke Sundquist (*Anders*); Björn Bjelvenstam (*Viktor*); Jullan Kindahl (*Agda, Isak's factotum*); Ulf Johansson (*Isak's father*); Naima Wifstrand (*Isak's mother*); Yngve Nordwall (*Uncle Aron*); Sif Ruud (*Aunt Olga*); Gertrud Fridh (*Karin, Isak's wife*); Åke Fridell (*her lover*); Gunnar Sjöberg (*Sten Alman*); Gunnel Broström (*Berit, his wife*); Max von Sydow (*Henrik Åkerman*); Anne-Marie Wiman (*Eva, his wife*); Gunnar Olsson (*Bishop Jakob Hovelius*); Per Skogsberg, Per Sjöstrand, Gio Petré, Gunnel Lindblom, Göran Lundquist, Maud Hansson, Eva Norée, Lena Bergman & Monica Ehrling (*Isak's brothers & sisters*).

AWARDS: The magazine *FIB*: silver prize, prize for best musical score and medal for Ingrid Thulin's performance. Berlin (VIII, 1958): Grand Prix (Golden Bear) and FIPRESCI (Fédération Internationale de la Presse Cinématographique) prize for Victor Sjöström's performance and for his entire film career. Venice (XIX, 1958): FIPRESCI prize for the best film out of competition, shared with *Wedding and Babies*. Sølvklumpen, the prize of the Norwegian Exhibitors Association 1958. First place on the *New York Post* list 1959. National Board of Review Award 1959 for best actor (Victor Sjöström) and best foreign film. One of the ten best films on the *New York Herald Tribune* list 1959. One of the eight best foreign films on the *Time* list 1959. One of the ten best films on the *Saturday Review* list 1959. One of the ten best films on the Canadian Broadcasting Corporation list 1959. One of the seven best films on film historian John Springer's list 1959. Nastro d'Argento (Italy) 1960 for best foreign film. The prize of the Polish Film Critics' Association 1960 for best foreign film. David O. Selznick Silver Laurel 1961. Tenth place in the *Sight & Sound* international critics' poll for the best film of all time.

SYNOPSIS & COMMENTARY: The life of an individual projected against a widened background of Swedish reality, with the present and past merged into a single dramaturgical form: this was the subject of Bergman's next film. *Wild Strawberries* is the story of one day in the life of Professor Isak Borg. This day, like the midnight sun, like the last night in the life of Strindberg's Miss Julie, contains the riddle of life, the riddle of a human being who at the end of his road can see himself in the new perspective.

Old Isak Borg, a doctor, wakes up one morning from a nightmare. He has had a dream of his own death, in which he wandered along the ghastly streets of a depopulated town and saw a hearse driving his own corpse. Later that day, Borg travels from Stockholm to Lund where he is to receive the title of doctor honoris causa. His daughter-in-law Marianne comes along. She is the childless, unhappy wife of Evald Borg, also a doctor, who lives in Lund. Marianne resents her wealthy father-in-law's indifference to his own son's financial worries. Her frank accusations give the old man the first doubts about himself. They stop the car near the place where Borg had spent his vacations with his family. There is a strawberry glade, the site of his first romance. It was there that Isak, refused by Sara, went ahead and married another woman. Isak becomes lost in his thoughts. Suddenly a young girl shows up with her two boyfriends. She imposes herself, bluntly asking for a lift.

They all drive on and happen to pick up a middle-aged married couple, the Almans, who have just had a car accident. These two have such a bad quarrel in the car that Marianne makes them get out and leaves them on the highway on their own.

The next stop is on Vättern Lake where Isak and Marianne visit the Professor's 96-year-old mother. Marianne is affected by the cold atmosphere of the reunion of mother and son.

Then Marianne takes the wheel. Isak dozes off again and in his half-sleep remembers his relationship to Sara and the failure of his own marriage. This is a kind of continuation of his early-morning dream; surrealistic images again question his value as both a human being and a doctor. Borg meets Alman at an imaginary exam. Alman takes him along to a love tryst between Isak's long-dead wife and her lover.

In the evening the celebrations are held at the university. When they are over, Isak Borg goes to sleep peacefully, having reached the conclusion that the recapitulation of his own life made earlier that day will allow him to reevaluate the norms of his behavior and to become reconciled with himself and the others.

Wild Strawberries, a film unanimously acknowledged as Bergman's top achievement (the Golden Bear prize in Berlin, 1958), was the director's last venture into creating an impressively complicated formal construction. Masterfully blending the past and present, Bergman again applied Alf Sjöberg's method; Isak Borg of the present day observes his own past, seen within the same frame. The same actors play the young hitchhikers and the friends of Isak's youth. By referring to the narrative convention that was used in *The Phantom Carriage* and by casting Victor Sjöström, then aged 78, in the main role, Bergman combined live tradition with contemporaneity, thus paying a unique tribute to the past.

The wild strawberry glade, which sometimes symbolized virginity in Northern iconography, has now become the synonym of memories and sites people like to revert to, and the Art Cinemas network organized in Sweden by SF a few years after the film was distributed was named Smultronstället.

The young girl to whom Professor Borg gives a lift (ABOVE) . . . makes him remember his own youth at the strawberry glade (BELOW).

ABOVE: Sten Alman and his wife Berit, just before their terrible quarrel in the car. BELOW: Surrealistic dreams question Borg's value as a scientist and human being.

ABOVE: Professor Borg receives his honorary degree. BELOW: Marianne and her father-in-law finally become friends.

Biographies and Critical Portraits of the Directors

Ingmar Bergman was born in Uppsala on July 14, 1918. His father, a clergyman, became chaplain to the King in Stockholm. Religion and ethical problems often form the main subjects in Bergman's films, as they do in the plays he has directed in the theater.

The best-known and most acclaimed Swedish director since Stiller and Sjöström, Bergman started his career working with amateur university players in Stockholm in the late Thirties. From 1940 to 1942 he was an assistant stage director at the Stockholm Opera House. From 1944 to 1946 he was the managing director and a stage director of the Helsingborg Municipal Theater, and from 1946 to 1949 first stage director of the Göteborg Municipal Theater. His directorial career continued at the Malmö Municipal Theater from 1953 to 1960 and at the Royal Dramatic Theater in Stockholm from 1960 to 1976 (as chief until 1966).

Throughout his years as a film director, he has constantly returned to the stage, generally directing such older and modern classic authors as Strindberg, Ibsen, Anouilh, Williams, Chekhov and Molière. His film work started in 1940 with screenwriting at Svensk Filmindustri. Bergman soon began directing his own scripts. In the Fifties and Sixties he directed a number of masterpieces with the help of talented directors of photography and carefully chosen performers. In 1969 he formed his own production company, Cinematograph, and since then has very often produced his own films as well. Considered as one of the few geniuses in the motion-picture industry, he has received most of the awards existing today, including several ''Oscars.'' In 1970 he also received the Irving Thalberg Memorial Award.

For many years Bergman declined offers to work abroad. In 1976, however, in an altercation with the Swedish tax authorities, he moved to West Germany, where he was engaged as director at the Residenz Theater in Munich until 1982. Since leaving Sweden, he has produced his films abroad through his German production company, Personafilm. He returned in 1981 to make a new Swedish movie, *Fanny and Alexander.*

Through the years, his films have become increasingly more profound, probing ever more deeply into human psychology and emotions, often so intensely as to shock the audience. He is particularly famed for his understanding of the female soul. Nevertheless, Bergman still directs comedies, documentaries and even operas, in addition to psychological dramas. Some of his scripts have been published in several languages.

Bergman's tremendous importance for the modern film art cannot be overestimated, although it took him a long time to achieve international acclaim, and even longer to be recognized at home. His first films, strongly influenced by French poetic realism, were unsuccessful commercially, but his position was consolidated by his two consecutive prizes at Cannes, for *Smiles of a Summer Night* in 1956 and for *The Seventh Seal* in 1957. *The Devil's Wanton* (1949), considered his first important work, although it received international distribution only considerably later, conveys in a brief compass some of the problems Bergman was later to treat not only from the narrow existentialist point of view, but within a broadened exploration of the human condition. His most important films are *The Seventh Seal* and *Wild Strawberries*, the former disguising a thoroughly modern set of problems in the form of a medieval morality play, the latter creatively continuing Alf Sjöberg's experiments with filmic treatment of time and space. Throughout his career Bergman has pursued several subject lines that treat ultimate human problems: birth, in *Brink of Life* (Nära livet); death, in *Wild Strawberries* and *The Seventh Seal*; the situation of the artist in society, in *The Magician* (Ansiktet), *The Naked Night* and *The Passion of Anna* (En passion); faith and the silence of God, in *Winter Light* (Nattvardsgästerna) and *The Silence* (Tystnaden). The religious preoccupations seemed to be central in Bergman's production, and were harshly criticized by the younger Swedish filmmakers, Bo Widerberg in particular. But there are some critics who consider that these films on religious motifs are not really foreign to a humanistic confrontation of man with man, and who read in his more recent films, from *Persona* (1965) on, a new approach, filmically more ascetic and less effect-seeking than before, but psychologically far- and deep-reaching. Actually Bergman is less convincing when handling very modern, concrete problems straightforwardly, such as the war in *Shame* (Skammen), 1968, and more faithful to himself when he remains in his geometrically limited human landscape, concentrating on just a few significant characters.

Hasse Ekman was born in Stockholm on September 10, 1915. His father was the celebrated actor Gösta Ekman. Hasse's acting debut was at the Folkan Theater in Stockholm in 1932; he went to study in Hollywood in 1935. He worked for SF from 1936 to 1939 and from 1953 to 1964, for Terrafilm from 1940 to 1945 and from 1948 to 1952; and for Europa Film in 1946 and 1947. He acted and directed for the Intima Teatern in Stockholm from 1951 to 1954 and from 1960 to 1964. Since the late Sixties he has lived in Spain, doing occasional theater productions in Stockholm (mostly revues at the Folkan).

A prolific actor and director, Hasse Ekman was one of the most promising Swedish filmmakers of the Forties and early Fifties, when he was considered to be just as serious and capable as Ingmar Bergman. Both directors were impressed and influenced by the tradition of French poetic realism—especially seen in Ekman's *Wandering with the Moon* and *Change of Trains*. His comedies and dark dramas (*The Suicide*) show stylistic accomplishment and a pessimistic undertone; though not profoundly gloomy, Ekman was rather sarcastic and free of romantic illusions. His inside reports from the elegant world of Stockholm society were a kind of bitter confrontation with his own background and traditions.

Arne Mattsson was born in Uppsala on December 2, 1919. Educated in business and engineering, he entered film production as an assistant director and scriptwriter for the small company Lux-Film.

His somewhat exaggerated reputation in the Fifties, when he was ranked as the third best Swedish director after Sjöberg and

Bergman, was based on some good literary adaptations, such as *Salka Valka*, 1954; on the poetic war movie *The Bread of Love* (Kärlekens bröd), 1953; and, most of all, on *One Summer of Happiness*, one of the biggest Swedish box-office hits all over the world, launching the whole wave of healthy and natural nude eroticism. This film, quite innocent from the modern point of view, was in fact a very poetic defense of clean and true love.

Mattsson's main preoccupation in the late Fifties and Sixties was the mass production of sensational movies, such as a series about detective Hillman, a mediocre attempt to copy the style of *The Thin Man*. These films became progressively more commercial, and acquired a more and more violent character. Mattsson's artistic decadence—his last film of value was *Woman of Darkness* (Yngsjömordet, literally: The Murder at Yngsjö), 1966—was widely observed by Swedish critics, to whom the director dedicated one of his latest works, the metafilm *Anne and Eve, the Erotics* (Anne och Eve, de erotiska), 1970.

Gustaf Molander was born in Helsinki on November 18, 1888, and died in Stockholm on June 20, 1973. His father, Harald Molander, was a theatrical producer at the Svenska Teatern in Helsinki, and in 1909 Gustaf became an actor there. He had studied acting at the Royal Dramatic Theater from 1907 to 1909 (from 1921 to 1926 he was a director at the same school). He was active in Stockholm theaters: the Intima Teatern from 1911 to 1913 and the Royal Dramatic Theater from 1913 to 1926. He entered filmmaking as a scriptwriter.

With his sixty-four features Gustaf Molander was the most prolific Swedish director up to the present. He took an active part in creating Swedish film history during almost all of its vicissitudes: writing scripts for Sjöström and Stiller; trying to uphold their classic tradition in the later Twenties (adaptations of Selma Lagerlöf's *Jerusalem*); assuming the artistic lead in the Thirties with his resourceful and elegant comedies and dramas; and working alongside the most committed Swedish directors during the revival of the greatness of Swedish film art with such anti-Nazi pictures as *Ride Tonight!* (Rid i natt!), 1942; *There's a Fire Burning* (Det brinner en eld), 1943; and —last but not least— *The Word* (Ordet), 1943. His career in the late Forties and Fifties, however, did not remain at the same high level. His big-budget remakes of classics did not repeat the artistic success of Stiller's versions, which had been scripted by Molander himself.

Not the least of Molander's merits was that of assisting Swedish stars when they were on the threshold of their international careers; Greta Garbo studied in his acting studio, and Ingrid Bergman became a star in his films in the late Thirties (he refused to follow her to Hollywood, preferring filmmaking in his native country) and starred in his last movie, *Stimulantia*, 1967. Molander was a director with a firm hand and a cultivated, though hardly modernistic, taste.

Alf Sjöberg was born in Stockholm on June 21, 1903, and died there on April 17, 1980. He attended an acting school at the Royal Dramatic Theater from 1923 to 1925 and performed there during the two following years. He made foreign tours, worked for radio and, from 1930 until his death, was the chief director of the Royal Dramatic Theater.

Sjöberg's reputation in the Forties and Fifties was based on some widely discussed films, such as *Miss Julie* (awarded the Grand Prix at Cannes in 1951), and on his tremendous contribution to the renewal of the Swedish cinema during World War II with films, such as *Life at Stake* and *Torment*, which mirrored the unique mood and tensions of those transitional years when Europe's destiny was at stake, or which—like *The Road to Heaven*—were direct links to the older Swedish film tradition. In his long creative career, Sjöberg used different stylistic patterns, but his indebtedness to Expressionism seems to be clear, while his major contribution to the development of film language is undoubtedly his device of showing in the same frame two actions that in "reality" are widely separated in time and/or space. These experiments were used creatively in *Miss Julie* and *The Judge* (Domaren), 1960, but more self-imitatively in his more recent *The Island* (Ön), 1966. Some critics have related Sjöberg's style to his stage experience (which was pursued more uninterruptedly than his film work), and have found this style not truly cinematic.

Victor Sjöström (in his international career, also known as Seastrom) was born in Silbodal on September 20, 1879, and died in Stockholm on January 3, 1960. His mother, Lisen Hartman, had been an actress in her youth. Sjöström, further influenced by his uncle, Victor Hartman, himself an actor, chose the same profession. His first engagement came in 1896 and until 1899 Sjöström toured with Swedish-language theaters in Finland. Even before 1912 and his contract with Svenska Bio, Sjöström proved to be a very versatile actor with a broad scale and big possibilities. He was also a stage manager and theatrical producer. Even during his film career, Sjöström gave occasional theatrical performances (in the Forties and Fifties). From 1923 to 1930 he was in Hollywood. From 1943 to 1949 he was artistic director of SF.

Sjöström's earliest films, as well as Stiller's, imitated the sensational, melodramatic Danish style. But he showed a strong involvement in social problems as well, as can still be seen in one of the few preserved early Swedish films of high quality, *Ingeborg Holm* (1913). After a hard crisis in both his artistic and his private life, Sjöström started in 1916 to make fewer but better pictures, and this influenced his producer Charles Magnusson's policy from then on. The first of these was *Terje Vigen*, directly followed by *The Outlaw and His Wife* and, a few years later, *The Phantom Carriage*. In his films Sjöström showed a very firm hand in revealing the primitive beauty of Northern nature, transforming it into a truly dramatic element, far beyond a mere background for the events of the plot. These qualities came to life with greatest force in his adaptations of novels by Selma Lagerlöf, which he treated with exemplary delicacy and fidelity, combining literary tradition with the strong impact of location shots, chiefly made in the wilds of Lapland.

Sjöström's Hollywood career was more successful than Stiller's; in his best pictures made there, one can still discern his previous style, as for instance in his American masterpiece *The Wind* (1928). Sjöström, who directed only three sound pictures, developed a new acting career for himself in later years, and in his last performance—in Ingmar Bergman's *Wild Strawberries*, 1957— formed a living link between two great moments in Swedish film art.

Mauritz Stiller was born in Helsinki on July 17, 1883, and died in Stockholm on November 8, 1928. His parents were of Russian-Jewish origin, and his father worked as an army musician. Educated in Helsinki, Stiller held down various jobs, and from 1899 worked as an extra and a bit player in various repertory groups. His tour to Sweden in 1904 enabled him to avoid being drafted into the Russian army. From 1907 to 1910 he was with the Swedish Theater in Helsinki, afterwards permanently in

Stockholm as both actor and director. In 1910 he became the manager and director of the famous avant-garde Lilla Teatern.He joined Svenska Bio as director and actor in 1912. In 1924 he traveled to Istanbul with his star Greta Garbo, but they never shot the film that had been planned. Then, via Berlin, he proceeded to Hollywood, where he signed up with MGM on July 1, 1925; later he was on Paramount's payroll. He returned to Stockholm at the end of 1927 to stage a theatrical production.

Stiller and Sjöström are the two outstanding representatives of Swedish film during its artistically and financially greatest period, 1916–1924. Stiller is considered less sober than Sjöström, less influenced by classic Swedish literature, less close to the national tradition. Nevertheless, his masterpiece, *Sir Arne's Treasure*, is regarded as one of the two or three best Swedish films of the period, and both *The Song of the Scarlet Flower* (Sången om den eldröda blomman) and *The Atonement of Gösta Berling* are visually very strong pictures, displaying the beauty of Scandinavian nature and constructing the plot around several magnificently and emotionally played characters. Stiller's approach to literary classics (especially novels by Selma Lagerlöf) can be called rather free, but he never indulged in frivolity except when shooting his own comedy scripts (frequently written in collaboration with Gustaf Molander and Ragnar Hyltén-Cavallius). The best of these sophisticated comedies with their lavish settings in high society was *Erotikon*, which influenced Ernst Lubitsch as he was developing his famous "touch." Stiller's American period was largely unsuccessful; he could not cope with the requirements of the Hollywood studio system. His place in film history is nevertheless firm, based on both of his stylistic trends, dramas played against the violent background of Northern nature and elegant indoor comedies.

Arne Sucksdorff was born in Stockholm on February 3, 1917. The son of a merchant, he graduated from high school in 1936 and then briefly studied zoology and painting (with Otte Sköld). His instructor in stage work at the Reimannschule in Berlin in 1937 was Rudolf Klein-Rogge, famous for his work in numerous Fritz Lang films. Sucksdorff's first attempts as a photographer won him prizes at several exhibitions. He began his film activity as a semiamateur documentary maker, soon getting commissions from SF. In the mid-Sixties he left Sweden for South America and married an Indian woman (an earlier marriage had been to Astrid Bergman, herself a well-known nature photographer).

Arne Sucksdorff's travels with his camera to forests and mountains in Sweden, rivers in India and jungles in South America demonstrate his urge to escape urban civilization, which he distrusts, and to create a visual alternative to it. Nevertheless, up to the mid-Sixties he had always come back to his native soil, but at that point Swedish film no longer seemed able to offer him creative work. In his films, Sucksdorff has shown the cruel but inevitable rules of nature: *The Gull*, *A Divided World*. He is as much an ethnographer as a naturalist: *Moving On*, *Village in India* (Indisk by). His attempts at depicting city life were not numerous although fully satisfactory: *Rhythm of the City*, *My Home Is Copacabana*. But he has always preferred to stick to the wilderness; at most, he would mix documentary with some slight, mostly improvised fictionalization. His only attempt at total fiction, using professional actors—*The Boy in the Tree* (Pojken i trädet), 1961—was a total failure.